Lost and Found

MY STORY OF HEARTBREAK AND HOPE

Toni Street

WITH SOPHIE NEVILLE

ALLEN&UNWIN
SYDNEY・MELBOURNE・AUCKLAND・LONDON

First published in 2021

Allen & Unwin
Level 2, 10 College Hill
Auckland 1011, New Zealand
Phone: (64 9) 377 380

Email: info@allenandunwin.com
Web: www.allenandunwin.co.nz

83 Alexander Street
Crows Nest NSW 2065, Australia
Phone: (61 2) 8425 0100

A catalogue record for this book is available
from the National Library of New Zealand

ISBN 978 1 98854 773 2

Design by Megan van Staden
Cover photograph by Monty Adams
Hair and makeup by Lisa Matson
Styling by Lulu Wilcox

Set in 12/18 pt Adobe Caslon Pro
Printed and bound in Australia by McPhersons Printing Group

10 9 8 7 6 5 4 3

To Mum and Dad,
for showing us what true courage is.

Contents

Twins

'Stephen's had an accident,' Mum says over the phone.

    'Is he okay? How bad is it?' I ask.

'It's bad, Tones.' Her voice breaks. 'He's died.'

It is 8 a.m. on 7 January 2002 and my life splits into two.

My brother's death becomes a seismic marker in my life — there's the time before he died, and the time after. Twenty years on and I still view my life in those two distinct parts.

I am eighteen. I have just finished seventh form (year 13) and I'm meant to be heading off to university in four weeks' time. This can't be happening. Stephen can't be dead, he's only fourteen; he has his whole life to live. And my parents, my poor parents. They have already lost two children — they won't survive this. I have to get home.

Friends scramble around me and somehow I'm on a plane heading from Christchurch to New Plymouth. I'm supposed to be playing cricket today for the Central Districts women's team. I am absolutely not meant to be flying home to my family in tatters.

The flight is a blur. My cousin Brad is sitting next to me, but I can't talk because I feel as if I'm suffocating. I don't know how he got there or why he's on this flight. I can barely breathe; the world is closing in on me.

The plane touches down. Everyone else is standing up, waiting to disembark. I have never felt so desperate to get off a plane in my life, but at the same time I've never been so terrified of what I'm about to face.

My family is inside the terminal waiting for me. But what even is my family without Stephen? My adorable, shy, beautiful little brother who wouldn't hurt a fly. This cannot be true.

Suddenly I'm up on my feet and I have to get off.

'Let me off the plane!' I want to scream, but I say nothing. The queue is moving now and I'm walking across the tarmac. The doors slide open and, oh my god, there they are. Mum, Dad and my little sister Kirsty, who is only eleven. They're all holding onto each other in a strange sort of huddle and they look different. Shellshocked. I run to them and they open their arms to me. We're all sobbing now, even Dad.

'I'm here, I'm here, I'm here,' I say. We stay in that group hug for the longest time. People are probably staring at us, but I don't care. My brother has died. Nothing else matters.

'It will be okay,' I promise, knowing it won't. How could it ever be okay when my parents have just lost a third child and Kirsty and I have lost our only brother?

One of Mum's biggest hopes for her children was that they would never know the grief she has lived with for most of her life. But now that Stephen has died, that hope is over for Kirsty and me. And the grief is all-consuming. Now I know why Mum describes grief as a burden, because there's definitely a weight to the feeling and you can't just shake it off.

Even now, twenty years on, I feel it. It's like an invisible cloak draped around my shoulders. Some days it's heavier than others, but it's always there. It touches everything I do and it's everywhere I go. How long are you supposed to be sad? I still don't know the answer, but I have learnt you can grieve and live at the same time. It took me a long time to accept that.

I have spent most of my adult life trying to make sense of what my parents went through and how they survived. Because Stephen was not their first loss. This book is not *my* story, it's *ours*. Writing about it is my way of honouring my parents and their experience. But this is not a 'misery memoir'; my family are some of the most joyful people you could meet. And that's the thing: when you've experienced loss like ours, life's good stuff is amplified. Love is deeper and colours are brighter.

But man, I miss my little brother. He'd love my kids. The girls, Juliette and Mackenzie, and his miracle nephew, Lachie, who was born with so many of his Uncle Stephen's traits — beautiful olive skin, dark brown eyes and the kindest nature. Sometimes Mum does a double-take when she sees him. 'Gosh, you're like your Uncle Stephen,' she'll murmur as she tucks Lachie into bed. 'Absolutely perfect.'

But I guess a book should start at the beginning, so let's go back to the day I was born, at Taranaki Base Hospital on 8 September 1983. My parents, Wendy and Geoff Street, were babies themselves: Mum 23 and Dad 27, newly married and at the start of what they were sure would be a happy life of farming and family.

They were childhood sweethearts who had met through their own parents, who were friends and golfing companions. After they got married they took over the Street family dairy farm. It wasn't huge — 180 acres with 160 cows — but it was big enough to keep Dad busy, and there was nowhere else they wanted to raise their future children.

The newlyweds had their loved ones close, in every sense of the word, because Dad's parents, Nana Joyce and Grandad Bert, lived just across the paddock, and Mum's parents, Nana June and Grandad Bob, lived five minutes away in the other direction.

My family were, and still are, what you'd call classic salt-of-the-earth people whose lives revolved around sport, the weather, their livestock and their close-knit community of neighbours, family and friends. Eggs, casseroles and baking were shared around, and kids roamed freely between houses. Rolling green hills dotted with pockets of native bush stretched as far as the eye could see. And it was also only a fifteen-minute drive to town, so we felt like we had the best of both worlds.

It was the early 1980s and Mum's biggest dream was to fill the house with kids and to be there for them, no matter what. She's a born homemaker, my mum, and she and Dad were set on giving us the best childhood they possibly could.

As far as I was concerned there was no better place on earth to grow up. We had the hills to explore, animals to play with, creeks to go eeling in, and a home that was always open to friends and cousins, who roamed as freely as we did. When I think back to our childhood on the farm, I appreciate it even more now that I realise how lucky we were to have all that space and freedom.

Even though we grew up in the shadow of loss and sadness, us kids were largely sheltered from it. We were completely wrapped up in our own carefree, happy little lives.

Something a lot of people don't know about me is that I am a twin. I have no real memories of my twin brother, Lance, though, because he died when we were just eighteen months old.

Before getting pregnant with us, Mum knew pretty much nothing about babies. She was totally naïve about what she was getting herself into. But Lance and I were born safe and well at 38 weeks, and Dad said it felt like winning Lotto — a boy and a girl in one hit.

Lance was born first, then I came along nine minutes later. I weighed 5.5 pounds (2.5 kilograms), slightly less than Lance, who was 6 pounds 15 ounces (3.1 kilograms). Back then, new mums stayed in the maternity hospital for up to a week after giving birth, and Mum was kept in even longer because Lance had mild jaundice. Even though I was the smaller twin, I was stronger and healthier from the get-go. I was noisier and more demanding, too, Mum said, always desperate to be involved in everything.

Lance was the laid-back one, happy kicking on a mat on the floor while I insisted on being carried everywhere. There's a home video shot when we were about ten months old that Mum says sums up our relationship perfectly — two little babies sitting side by side holding ice-creams. Suddenly I reach over, help myself to Lance's one and demolish them both. Lance looks at me hoeing into his ice-cream, then gives a resigned look to the camera as if to say 'Oh well, what can you do?'

The first sign that Lance might not be as healthy as he should be was when he was about a month old and developed a skin infection near his tummy button, right where the old-fashioned nappies fastened with a safety pin. It started off as a little patch of blisters, which the doctor told Mum was probably just nappy rash.

It didn't clear up, though, and Mum began to worry when she noticed Lance's general health going downhill. He was sleeping more, wasn't feeding as well, and just seemed out of sorts. She took him back to the doctor several times, but was always sent home with a new skin cream to try and told not to worry. A visiting Plunket nurse eventually raised the alarm. By now the skin was badly infected — and, scarily, Lance was kind of floppy. On the Plunket nurse's advice Mum and Dad rushed him to hospital, where he ended up staying for a week. It turned out the rash was a severe staphylococcal infection for which he urgently needed IV antibiotics and fluids.

Mum remained in the hospital with Lance, and I stayed at home with Nana June. Dad had to keep milking the cows, so he would rush home from the milking shed to see me, then go into the hospital. Our separation meant Mum had to stop breastfeeding me, which was upsetting for her, but she was determined to keep me away from hospital germs. It was bad enough having one baby in there; she didn't want me anywhere near the place.

Once Lance was sent home he seemed to go from strength to strength. Mum and Dad loved watching us interact, rolling around on the floor, cooing at each other in what all parents of twins seem to think is a secret language between the babies.

However, as the months went by, Lance seemed to pick up coughs and colds and little bugs that I just didn't catch. Then at six months he developed a throat infection that really knocked him around. When his fever peaked at 40 degrees Celsius, Mum took him to hospital and refused to leave until they found out what was going on. After a couple of days of no improvement he was transferred to the Princess Mary Hospital for Children in Auckland.

The Princess Mary (now Starship Children's Hospital) was the place for the sickest children, so Mum and Dad were terrified. It was clear this was a lot more than just a throat infection. Lance was subjected to a barrage of tests that no baby should ever have to endure — blood tests, X-rays, scans and (something Mum will never forget) a lumbar puncture and bone-marrow sample taken without anaesthetic. 'Don't worry, Mrs Street, he won't remember it,' a doctor reassured her as he pushed a huge needle into Lance's femur and hip.

Lance was eventually diagnosed with a rare genetic condition called Kostmann Syndrome. There was no Google back then, so my parents had to rely on the scant information they were given at the hospital. They were told the syndrome was a genetic condition characterised by a predisposition to life-threatening bacterial infections, which meant he had a reduced life expectancy of about four years. To add to my parents' misery, they were told any future children also had a one-in-four chance of having the condition.

Mum and Dad were reeling but they brought Lance home to the farm, determined to make his short life a happy one. Deep in her heart, Mum never quite accepted the Kostmann Syndrome diagnosis. When Lance seemed to make a good recovery at home, gaining strength and avoiding major infections over the next few months, her hopes rose.

'He's a fighter; I knew he'd come right,' she would tell her friends.

For three months Lance remained healthy and Mum and Dad thought their problems were behind them. But it didn't last. At nine months old he developed a cough and fever. It was another throat infection, so he was sent back up to the Princess Mary Hospital.

It turned out Mum was right: Lance didn't have Kostmann Syndrome, the doctors decided. It was worse — he had a rare form of acute myeloid leukaemia, a type of blood and bone marrow cancer. My parents listened in disbelief as they were told their baby needed aggressive chemotherapy, and even with that he was unlikely to live longer than another two years.

They were crushed. While Dad focused on the practicalities of treatment options, and quizzed doctors on what they could do to make Lance more comfortable, Mum went into full-on denial and refused to give up hope of a cure. She clung to stories of miracles, and went to church and prayed that her little boy would be saved.

I think my parents were forever scarred by watching their baby go through cancer treatment. Mum says she'll never forget the sound of the 'bloods trolley' rattling down the corridor for the daily blood tests. Every child on the cancer ward would start crying because they knew what was coming. Even though he was so weak, Lance would try to hide his arms behind his back. He was covered in what Mum called his 'chemo rash', an angry redness that covered his tiny body from top to toe. She had to drape a kind of net over him to stop him from scratching himself raw. He was in agony and there was nothing anyone could do to help.

Mum was only 23, but she was growing up fast. She says it was during Lance's illness that she learnt to truly fight for her kids.

Dad lined up someone else to do the farm work so he could be in Auckland, and once again I stayed at home with Nana June. No wonder she always felt like a second mum to me; I just adored her. I even started calling her 'Mum'. That story was always told with a laugh, but now I'm a mother I can see how tough that must have been for Mum.

Even though she knew I was happy and healthy at home, she hated leaving me and longed to have her twins together. It felt all wrong that we were apart, but she knew that a children's hospital then was not the place for a healthy nine-month-old.

After about a month of treatment Lance was well enough to come home. His doctors didn't think he would have a long life, but my parents never gave up hope that he would be a miracle child for whom the cancer would not return.

As you can imagine, our first birthday was a huge milestone, and even though Lance was weak from the treatment, there are photos of him smiling and looking happy. Mum and Dad held a party at home, where apparently I constantly gave Lance kisses and stayed by his side.

Even though he seemed to be doing well, he continued to have regular blood tests to monitor where he was at.

On 8 January 1985 Mum and Dad took Lance and me

to the beach with another family for a day out. I was only sixteen months old, but I swear I can remember parts of that beautiful summer day. My parents' mates were teaching them to windsurf and there was a gaggle of kids playing on the beach, wading in the shallows and building sandcastles.

Dad went home early to milk the cows, and when Mum pulled up in the car with Lance and me a couple of hours later she saw Dad walking towards the garage to meet us. He was crying. 'The latest blood results just came through,' he said. 'Lance has relapsed.'

Everyone knew this was likely to be the beginning of the end.

Mum, Dad and Lance were back off to Auckland, where the oncologist gave them the devastating news that their little boy had between two and six weeks to live. My parents were heartbroken. How could it be true when just a few days ago he had been running around on the beach?

They took Lance home, and for the next month life revolved around their sick baby, who was fading away in front of their eyes. Almost overnight he became a bag of bones, his skin almost translucent. He had no energy and spent most of his days lying in someone's arms or propped up on the sofa with pillows, while I played on the floor in front of him. The contrast between the two of us was a cruel and constant reminder of the reality they were facing. Life versus death in one set of twins.

In those final weeks with Lance, Mum and Dad did everything they could think of to make him happy. He loved ducks, so every day they wrapped him up in blankets and took him to feed the ducks at the pond on the farm. They bought him musical toys, mini cars and trucks and Care Bears, and pretty much anything they thought he might like. Every little smile he was able to give brought them so much joy, but there was no avoiding the fact that he was getting sicker and weaker each day.

He was also in pain, yet my parents were effectively left on their own to nurse their dying baby. There was no hospice support back then and only occasional visits from a local nurse, so it was up to them to administer his morphine. Mum was completely overwhelmed by it all. Thank god they had my grandparents nearby, especially as they also had me to look after.

The night before Lance died, something special happened. He was so ill he had hardly opened his eyes that day, and everyone knew it wouldn't be long. But as Dad carried him off to bed he looked over his shoulder at Mum, grinned and blew her a raspberry. It meant everything to Mum, because it showed her that, despite everything, he still had his sense of humour and he was still able to smile. She went to bed that night feeling more at peace than she had in weeks.

The next morning, when Mum went to see Lance in his cot, she noticed his breathing had changed. It was shallower and faster than normal. She gently tucked him into bed next to Dad and went to get me up. As she carried me into their bedroom Dad looked at her sadly and said, 'He's going . . .' So Mum joined them in bed, with Lance and me sandwiched between them, and they cuddled us close as his breathing became more erratic. After a little while Lance's eyes closed softly and he slipped away, nestled among his family.

Mum's and Dad's hearts were broken, but Lance's suffering was over.

My twin brother was farewelled in a quiet ceremony on the back lawn at home. Gathered around his heartbreakingly tiny coffin were Mum, Dad, me, the four grandparents, a couple of close friends and the local Anglican minister.

My parents got through it, but afterwards, when all the visitors had left and it was only us, Mum just wanted to disappear. Her baby had died and she wanted to go to bed and never get up. But she couldn't, because she had me. That's what she says saved her in the end — I was the reason she had to get up each day, put on her happy face and somehow try to accept what had happened. She struggled, though, because back then, particularly in rural New Zealand, there wasn't much support on offer. She had no one she felt she could talk to about how she was feeling. Even in her family there was a prevailing attitude of 'just get on with it'. It was how people coped.

She remembers emerging from the bedroom on the morning Lance died to find her father-in-law, my Grandad Bert, looking out the kitchen window. He turned to her and said, 'Well, there's a lot of work needs doing on this farm. The best thing you can do is get out and get stuck in.'

He was hurting, too, and he was a wonderful, loving man, but that was the only response he knew how to give.

Sometimes Mum would put me in the car and drive off, just to escape the memories at home. Every single day she cried for Lance. She missed him and longed for him, and when she looked at me she felt the loss all over again.

Like most newly married couples, Mum and Dad had no money. They had bought the farm the year before and mortgage interest rates soared to over twenty per cent. They couldn't afford to hire a worker so any milkings or days off were done by family and friends. No matter how devastated Dad felt, he still had to get up at 4.30 a.m. every day to milk and work twelve hours a day, seven days a week. It was very tough on him.

I remember very little of this now. I didn't have a clue what it all meant at the time, but I knew I was no longer a twin. People sometimes ask me whether I grew up with a sense that someone or something was missing. I'd love to say yes — I would love to feel Lance's presence in some way

— but the truth is that I was just too young to retain any memories.

The loss of Lance should have been the biggest tragedy for our family. But it was just the start.

Taranaki days

Now I was no longer a twin, Mum and Dad were determined to give me a new brother or sister as soon as they could. Even though I seemed untroubled by losing Lance, they were worried about the long-term impact of being separated from the baby I had been so connected to.

As far as they were concerned, the sooner they filled up the house with more kids, the sooner we would all feel better. So no one was surprised when Mum got pregnant shortly after Lance died, and everyone hoped this signalled the start of a happy new chapter for our family.

But very early on Mum started bleeding. The doctor kept telling her all was well, but deep down she had a horrible feeling that things were not right. How could they be when she was bleeding almost every day? She gained hardly any weight, and an early scan showed she had low amniotic fluid. For some baffling reason her GP remained unconcerned and did not refer her for further tests. Mum kept going back and asking for help, but none was given. At one point her doctor suggested she was being paranoid because of what she had been through with Lance.

Mum was furious. This had nothing to do with grief; she simply knew things were not right with her baby. She was only 25, but she had learnt a lot in the previous year. And yet she did not feel able to second-guess her GP. If the same thing happened now, a scan would have quickly revealed the problem. But back then, no one had a clue what was going on and no one seemed particularly interested in finding out.

Mum bled right up to 40 weeks, but this baby — my little sister Tracy Ann — hung in there until her due date of 10 April 1986. To my parents' relief, she weighed a healthy 3.6 kilograms and announced her arrival with a hearty scream. Mum finally allowed herself to believe that all was well. 'Maybe I *was* just paranoid,' she told herself. I remember holding my breath for that scream with all three of my babies, and it was the biggest relief when it came.

But a couple of minutes after she was born, while Mum was holding her, Tracy went as white as a ghost and then turned a terrifying shade of blue. Mum shouted for a nurse, who took one look at the limp little baby and hit the panic button. Suddenly sirens blared and doctors came running. A huge team worked to bring Tracy back to life before she was taken to the intensive care unit and placed on a ventilator.

Once more, my parents found themselves at the bedside of a very sick baby. It was through a haze of horror and disbelief that they were told their daughter had been born with no kidneys; she could not survive.

A year after burying a baby son, they were now saying goodbye to a daughter. My devastated parents were given a few hours to spend with Tracy before the machines were turned off. All the grandparents visited to say their goodbyes, and I was brought in, too, to meet my little sister. I have no memory of this either, but, fourteen hours after she was born, Tracy slipped away in the arms of my Nana Joyce.

Mum was angry. Angry about what had happened to her baby girl, furious with the doctors for not listening to her when she was pregnant, and in a state of shock that this had happened to her again. The final insult came when her GP, the one who had ignored her concerns, visited her in hospital after Tracy died. He patted her on the arm and said, 'Oh well, you've got through it before, you can do it again.'

Before Lance and Tracy, Mum had been a really positive person. Newly married, starting their little family, she and Dad had felt they had it all. A few short years later they were at rock bottom. Two children lost.

They held a small graveside service for Tracy at the local cemetery and she was laid to rest next to Lance, which I know gave my parents some comfort. Mum and Dad have always had a strong faith, and even after all they've been through they retain that faith. They cling to the idea that they'll see their children again, and I think that has kept them going in their darkest times.

Back then, Mum felt more alone and bereft than ever, and utterly dejected about her life. Dad, in the midst of his own grief, did his best to help, but his way of dealing with the tough stuff in life has always been through an unwavering positivity. He can find the light in any situation, and he has always refused to let sadness take over. This works well for him, but it has driven Mum crazy at times. There are moments in life when it's therapeutic to wallow or cry — and to feel that your sadness is being heard.

Thankfully, Mum found a support group for bereaved parents. There she met others who had been through similar experiences and survived. That showed her that she, too, would get through this. She's stubborn like that, and it has served her well.

So even though every instinct was to stay at home and hide from the world, Mum and Dad somehow picked up the pieces and carried on. They learnt that routine can pull you through the toughest times. Mum forced herself to keep doing the normal things, like taking me to playgroups, to the supermarket and out for walks with other mums.

It takes bravery to face the world through raw grief, and, although she might not realise it, Mum is one of the most courageous people I know. She says I gave her a reason to keep going, but ultimately it was she who made the decision to move forward. 'One foot in front of the other, Tones.' I don't know how many times I've heard her say that, but it became her mantra.

Even though they were scared, Mum and Dad wanted to keep trying for the happy household full of kids that they had dreamed of. A year later they were absolutely delighted to welcome a perfect little boy. Stephen William Street was born on 12 May 1987 after a happy, straightforward pregnancy.

I don't know how Mum managed to hold onto hope throughout that pregnancy, but she says that from the beginning she knew she was carrying a healthy baby. And when he arrived she felt a line had been drawn in the sand

— her life was back on track and she had a lot to be thankful for. Stephen's birth marked a new beginning.

I was only three and a half, but I clearly remember Nana June taking me to meet my little brother at Taranaki Base Hospital the day he was born. He was a gorgeous wee thing with his brown eyes and lovely olive skin, and Mum and Dad were so happy.

For a very long time they stayed that way.

Two years after Stephen was born my little sister Kirsty Ellen came along, which meant that finally my parents had the bustling, noisy, chaotic house they had always wanted. My most vivid memories of my childhood are happy ones. I loved the farm; I loved my family and friends. By the time I started at the local school, Bell Block Primary, it felt as if our family had healed.

Life revolved around the farm, school, friends and our family's big passion: sport. Stephen was the quietest of the three Street kids — he was happy to let the girls lead the way, traipsing along behind us, playing all the girly games we wanted and never complaining. Man, he was cute — Kirsty and I loved dressing him up in silly outfits, and we always gave him a cameo role in the shows we put on for Mum and Dad. They joked that Kirsty and I came out of the womb singing and dancing, but Stephen was the opposite. Where we were natural showoffs, he was more likely to be hiding behind Mum's legs. You might expect the oldest child to be the bossy one, but not in our family. Kirsty ruled the roost then, and she rules the roost now, too!

One of the ways Mum dealt with her sadness over Lance and Tracy was to throw herself into our lives. She wanted us to have every opportunity Lance and Tracy had missed out on, and she was almost frenetic about signing us up to things, taking us to every possible activity and making sure we never missed a chance to try something new. We did dancing and singing classes, and every sport imaginable. I don't know how we fitted it all in.

Sport was the focal point. By the time I was seven I belonged to the local East End Surf Club, played netball and cricket, and was involved in athletics. We were a competitive family, there's no two ways about it. From early on our parents made it clear they had high expectations. It wasn't all about winning, though; it was about putting in maximum effort. We learnt that if you trained for something and put the work in, you would be rewarded with good results. They pushed us to be the very best we could be; there was a big focus on striving. Social sport was never really an option for the Street kids.

'You've got to have a winner,' Dad said. 'There's no point playing if you're not out to win.'

If you met Dad you would think he's the nicest person in the world. He's gentle and kind and loves nothing more than a good natter over a beer with anyone he meets. He never gets angry — I'd say I've only ever heard him raise his voice once or twice. He's calm, generous and wouldn't hurt a fly. But the minute you get the man on a sports field or a golf course he morphs into someone entirely different. He becomes fixated on winning and he'll fight to the death. And it's not just sport — even a family game of cards (usually 500 in our family) or Monopoly takes a serious turn when Dad's involved. His eyes narrow, his focus sharpens, and coming second just isn't an option.

So perhaps it's no surprise I took winning seriously when I started getting into sport. It turned out I was pretty good at cross country and athletics, which delighted Dad because there was nothing he loved more than seeing one of his kids at the front of the pack.

Most nine- and ten-year-olds didn't train for these events. Some turned up to the start line in jandals and tutus, but not me. For weeks before the annual school cross country, Dad, my self-appointed coach, would haul me out of bed at 6 a.m. and have me out running up and down hills on the farm, or a five-kilometre loop on the country roads. 'That's how you get good, Tones. It's all about hard work.' This went on for years, with me cursing him under my breath.

On race day, when all the other parents (the normal ones) would wait at the finish line, ready to cheer whenever their kids made it to the end, Dad would run parts of the race alongside me, yelling encouragement, dishing out advice — 'You're going to have to pick up the pace, Tones; she's closing in on you!' He was relentless, but it did the trick.

When I got to Highlands Intermediate in 1995 I came

second to a girl who was a year older. I started eyeing up victory the following year — there was a big shiny cup for the winner and I desperately wanted my name on that silverware. But a new threat arrived in the form of a tall, blonde girl named Sophie Stephens. She had just moved to Taranaki from Auckland. I didn't know it at the time, but this willowy tween would become one of the most important people in my life.

When I first spotted her across the playground my immediate thought was 'Uh oh, she looks like she'll be good at cross country.'

I was right. I ended up winning the race that year, but I'm sure if my dad had trained Sophie she would have given me a real run for my money. Years later Dad would train us both to run two half-marathons together.

It took a while for our friendship to blossom, but when Sophie and I got to New Plymouth Girls' High in 1997 we became good mates. I think we gravitated towards each other because we had the same approach to life — we loved a challenge, and we encouraged each other to put our hands up for pretty much everything. We both had a sense of adventure, and neither of us were afflicted by any of the teenage angst or embarrassment that stops some kids from trying new things. If I said 'Shall we enter the talent quest?', she would say 'Let's do it!'

And she's still like that — why else would she offer to be a surrogate mother for her best friend's child? She's smart and unflappable, with a steely determination. Some people find Soph intimidating — she's strikingly beautiful with a model's figure and is good at anything she decides to do — but to those of us who know her she's the warmest, most generous friend, and she's been that way for me since we were kids. Once she lets you in, you're there for life. She always has your back.

Soon we were hanging out pretty much all the time and were regulars at each other's houses, along with our tight group of high-school girlfriends. Soph often spent entire weekends at our place, and I'd usually be found at hers after school, where we would hang out while we practised for Stage Challenge or got ready for a surf-club party. We spent so much time together she soon became like an extended member of my family, and it was the same for me at her house. Her parents, Martin and Karen, welcomed me into their home from the start.

It was around this time that I gave her the nickname Willow — not because she's willowy, although she is, but because one of our friends had a white cat called Sophie Willow and they kind of looked the same. So Willow she became, and the name has stuck. To my children now, Sophie has never been known as anything other than Aunty Willow.

After the cross-country effort, Dad identified a talent in

Sophie and took her for training sessions, too. He would drag us both down farm roads on his gruelling runs, and in sixth form Sophie and I decided to attempt our first half-marathon. Dad, a seasoned marathon runner, took his coaching role seriously of course, drawing up a training plan and making us stick to it. Even now Sophie says she can hear my dad's voice in her head when she's out for a run and approaching a hill. 'Keep your head down, don't look to the top, one foot in front of the other.' She's as passionate about exercise as he is, so they get along just fine.

Sophie's and my sporting relationship did have its low points, though. I accidentally broke her fingers once during a cricket 'friendly'. (I told you social sport was not my thing!) For some inexplicable reason Soph had decided batting without gloves was a good idea. Needless to say, I carried on with the cricket past intermediate and she didn't.

I worked hard at school, I got good marks and was turning out to be handy on the sports field, too. I made the first XI cricket team in third form, and got into the A netball team in my fourth-form year. At fourteen I was playing cricket for the Central Districts Under-21 team, and a year or two later I was selected for the Central Districts women's team. That was pretty exciting, but it was busy — long practices in the evenings and games away most weekends. I was one of the youngest in my teams, but I loved it. The older players took me under their wing.

Mum and Dad thrived on following my sport. They would pack up the car, load Kirsty and Stephen in the back, and the four of them would drive for hours to wherever I was playing to cheer me on from the sidelines. It was the same with netball. I played for my school team and also for the Taranaki Under-15s and Under-19s.

My parents were a huge part of my success. Dad helped so much with my training, taking me down to the cricket nets at any spare opportunity, and Mum coached my netball teams in the early years. They did the same for Stephen and Kirsty. Stephen would come to watch my netball, we would all go to his rugby games, and we were all there for Kirsty's hockey. We knew all the players in each team, so dinner-table discussions were always around who was playing what position and how they were performing. We bonded over sport; it was our shared family love. Kirsty or I would rush in from school and say 'Guess what happened today? So-and-so threw a wobbly and wouldn't go on the court!', and Stephen would say 'Oh that's so typical, she always does that!'

Mum and Dad's approach on the sidelines was pretty straightforward. If we played well they were proud, and if we didn't have a good game they were still proud but would talk us through how we could do better. But they never made us feel bad; it was about teaching us to play to our potential.

I reckon it's a Taranaki farming thing — there's no point doing something if you're not going to do it properly. We were brought up to push ourselves hard, and I'll be forever thankful for that work ethic they instilled in me.

During a club rugby game when I was about seven I took a nasty fall and hurt my arm. It was pretty sore and I wanted to leave the field. I looked over at Dad, who was our coach. 'You'll be right, carry on,' he shouted with an encouraging thumbs-up as he edged me back onto the field. A couple of minutes later I dropped to my knees in agony, and after a trip to A&E it turned out my arm was broken. Mum was so angry with him. 'She should never have played on,' she hissed as we drove home, my arm in a cast and Dad looking a bit sheepish.

Ten years later another incident on the rugby field ended in a much more serious injury. I was playing women's tackle rugby for Spotswood United and went to kick a loose ball. My shin collided with another girl's and apparently you could hear the crack all over the Tukapa Rugby Club. I collapsed to the ground with my leg bent badly mid-shin and was carted off to hospital, where they found I had snapped both my fibula and tibia virtually clean in half. I had to have metal rods and pins surgically inserted, and it was a long, hard road to recovery. My netball coach was pretty annoyed. She had never been a fan of my decision to play both codes, so that was the last rugby game I ever played.

I love having such invested parents. Their approach taught

me the importance of hard work and motivation, and that you have to work for the things you want in life. It's an attitude that set me up for life. I still try to put in the absolute most that I can, regardless of the task.

I am determined to be as involved in my own children's sport as my parents were with mine. I love coaching the girls' netball teams, but sometimes I can feel myself channelling my father and I give myself a little talking to. 'Chill out, Toni, they're only eight.'

I get huge joy from seeing my kids play sport, even if it does feel as if we've come full circle when we're carting them off to Saturday morning rugby and netball, lugging the gear bags, seeing our breath on those cold mornings on the sideline. The camaraderie of a team environment is such a special thing. I reckon it's only a matter of time before I introduce the 6 a.m. cross-country training . . .

By fifth form, Sophie and I were immersed fully in the surf lifesaving scene in New Plymouth, and in the summer months the surf lifesaving club at East End became our second home. We loved it down there. In the summer holidays we would start at 6 a.m. with squad swim training at the pool, followed by a 10.30 a.m. beach fitness session. We'd return to the beach at 5 p.m. for sprint training, then stay on for the club parties, which were a huge part of the appeal. It was intergenerational — my parents were involved with fundraising and the admin side, and Kirsty and Stephen were junior members. It was the best little community and such an awesome place to spend weekends.

Sophie and I felt pretty cool because we were often hanging out with much older kids. Mum and Dad were pretty relaxed about that sort of thing. They would give me a four-pack of RTDs to take to a party and trusted that I'd be sensible. Which I guess I was, most of the time. My school friends and I would usually start at my house for pre-drinks before heading off to a party, either at the surf club or in a hall someone had rented out. Hall parties were a big thing in rural New Zealand back then. You would pile in, drink your RTDs, dance to classic '90s hits and work out who was 'going out' with who before your mum or dad came to pick you up at the appointed time. It was the small-town teenage dream.

Because we lived rurally, my parents would always offer to be on drop-off and pick-up duty. Sophie and the rest of my tight group of girlfriends would often end up sleeping over at our place after parties. Mum and Dad always welcomed other kids; ours was one of those houses my friends knew they could visit any time. Mum never seemed to get tired of dishing up extra food or vacating the lounge while we rehearsed for yet another of our performances.

It wasn't just sport that I threw myself into throughout my school years — I also got into performing. In form one (year 7) I played the lead in a musical production called *Bats*. I played a police officer who was great at her job but struggled in her love life. To my horror I had to hold hands and sing a love song to my love interest. Doing that with a nerdy twelve-year-old boy was quite possibly the most cringe-worthy thing I had ever had to do; I still blush when I think about it.

I also played the clarinet (badly) in the orchestra, and took singing and dancing lessons. I'm sounding like a real Pollyanna now, but I was just one of those kids who wanted to do everything. I have no idea how I managed to fit it all in, but I expect it was because Mum was there, playing taxi-driver, packing my lunches and generally making sure I was living my best life. That's the thing about Mum. She never complained about not having her own time or career outside the house; saying she was 100 per cent happy devoting herself to us. Her sole objective was to ensure that we were happy and fulfilled our potential.

I was one of the only kids in our group to have my own car, in the form of the old family Subaru Legacy. I got my licence as soon as I turned fifteen and it was a godsend for my parents, who had spent half their lives carting me around to practices and rehearsals. They generously gave me their old car and, bless them, thought I would be delighted when they surprised me with a personalised number plate. It was in the days when 'da bomb' was a popular saying, but as that wasn't available they made do with 'Z BOMB'.

From that day forward I was known as the girl with the Z Bomb wheels, and the kids at school had a field day. It was punishing. The boys even started calling me Z Bomb. I was mortified, but I just had to own it. All I could do was laugh as the boys at the neighbouring high school yelled and jeered whenever I drove past.

Life was pretty idyllic and I think we felt kind of invincible, because as kids you never think things are going to go wrong. But in 2000 our beloved Nana June — Mum's mum, the one who had looked after me as a baby and been pretty much a second mother to us all — dropped dead suddenly of a heart attack. She was 62. We were shattered.

For Mum it brought back the horror of losing Lance and Tracy. Grief, her old friend, was back, and she was devastated with her mum no longer down the road. She was especially upset that Nana wasn't around to see me made head girl of New Plymouth Girls' High. My parents were so proud, and they knew it would have meant a lot to Nana, who always had such a special place in her heart for me after what we went through together when Lance was sick.

It was an utter blow to my Grandad Bob — he just wasn't the same after Nana died, and passed away a few years later. Within the following five years all four of my much-loved grandparents were gone.

Stephen

Like many teenage boys, Stephen loved sport and he loved hanging out with his mates. But he was happiest out on the farm with Dad. They were a tight duo. We all used to go out with Dad on the back of his quadbike, but it was Stephen who loved it the most. Every day after school he

LOST AND FOUND

would walk in the door, throw down his schoolbag and head out to see what Dad was up to

Stephen wasn't particularly academic; he struggled at school, and I know he found that doubly tough because schoolwork came quite easily to Kirsty and me. But he had other skills. He was a courageous little rugby player. He wasn't big, but he was wily and could outwit his opponents. He was amazing with his hands — skills honed by all those hours spent mucking around in the shed with Dad. He was a perfectionist, and he was driven. When he wanted something he would put his mind to it and spend as much time as he needed to make it happen.

I remember when he was desperate to get a cellphone, so he collected bottle caps to trade for money. It took a *lot* of bottle caps, but Stephen was determined. He had all the neighbours saving their bottle caps for him, too. And when he wanted a PlayStation he struck a deal with Mum and Dad that if he learnt his times tables they would buy him one. He just went for it; for months he practised and practised and eventually nailed it. He got his PlayStation.

We all remember the day he came home with his school report at the end of third form. He walked in the door and flopped on the couch face-down. Mum realised he was crying, but all he would say was 'I've done no good.' He had failed maths, which was meant to be his strongest subject. Mum picked him up and cuddled him like a baby, doing her

40

best to console him. She reminded him about all the things he was great at that other kids might not be. We didn't know what else to do. It was heartbreaking.

Then Mum told him about John Britten, the Christchurch motorcycle engineer who was dyslexic but had still managed to create the world's fastest motorbike. She told Stephen that perhaps he was dyslexic, too, and promised him 'we're gonna get it sorted'. She said she would buy him a copy of Britten's biography and read it to him. 'You will be so clever, Stephen, you could 100 per cent build a motorbike like that,' she told him. He looked up, his beautiful brown eyes sparkling, and said, 'Do you really think I could?' The idea that someone who struggled like him at school could still be successful filled him with hope.

'Yes! I know you could,' Mum said, and she meant it.

That summer had started so well. I finished my final year of school on an absolute high. I had loved being head girl, I got an A bursary and was excited about moving away from home. I had been awarded a sports scholarship to study at Lincoln University in Canterbury, and would train at New Zealand Cricket's High Performance Centre, which is attached to the campus.

It meant my university fees would be paid and I would play and train with the best resources in New Zealand. It was an amazing opportunity, and while the prospect of living away from home was a bit daunting, I felt reassured that Sophie and her boyfriend, Michael Braggins (who she would go on to marry), were moving south too, to study at the University of Canterbury. My boyfriend at the time, Rhys, was also going there.

I spent that final summer at home playing cricket for Central Districts, relaxing at the farm, doing plenty of socialising with family and friends, and hanging out at the surf club. I look back on those few weeks of holidays as a sort of utopia. Little did I know my world was about to implode.

Everything changed on the morning of 7 January 2002. I had been in Dunedin playing for the Central Districts cricket team and we had taken a very early flight back to Christchurch. Milling around at the airport as we waited for our bus to Lincoln, I had no idea that back home my family was breaking into a million pieces.

The night before had been much like any other back in Taranaki. Mum and Dad had friends over for dinner, and Stephen and Kirsty decided to have a sleepover in my bedroom. I had a queen bed, of which they were hugely jealous because they still had their little single beds, so occasionally they begged Mum to let them bunk in mine for the night when I was away playing cricket. Stephen always struggled to get to sleep, being a bit of a worrier, so he enjoyed sharing a room, and Kirsty just loved getting her own way with Mum.

When Mum went to tuck them in at about eleven o'clock they had built a pillow barrier down the middle of the bed and were arguing over who had the most room. Mum settled them down and pulled up the duvet, and then out of nowhere Stephen suddenly asked her about the John Britten book.

'Have you bought it yet, Mum?'

It had slipped her mind, but it hadn't slipped Stephen's.

Mum felt terrible. 'Sorry, darling, we'll go and buy it tomorrow, I promise.'

'Okay, Mum, night night. Love you.'

That was the last time she would see him alive.

The next morning Dad crept in at about six and got Stephen up to help him with the milking. The night before, Stephen had had a sore foot that was a bit swollen, so Mum had said, 'He's not going up to the shed like that.' But Dad, being Dad, thought, 'He'll be right.' Besides, he and Stephen wanted to play golf that morning so they were keen to get the jobs finished early.

Dad was busy milking and asked Stephen to jump on the quadbike and go and put out a bit of fencing in a paddock about 200 metres away. It was a totally normal sort of thing — Stephen knew the terrain and had been helping with jobs like fencing since he was little.

It should have been a quick job, and when Stephen hadn't returned after a while Dad started to wonder why not. He set off across the paddock on foot to find him. Maybe the bike had broken down, or he had run into trouble with the fence job.

As he came up over the top of a hill he saw him.

The quadbike was flipped on its back and Stephen was pinned underneath it. Dad broke into a sprint and managed to lift the quadbike off the lifeless body of his son. He knew immediately that Stephen had died, but he began CPR, desperately trying to pump life back into him. He could not accept this — no way was he taking another dead child home to Wendy. 'Come on, son, come on!'

The CPR wasn't working, so Dad scooped Stephen up into his arms and carried him back to the milking shed. All he could think was that he had to save him, he had to bring him back to life. He laid Stephen on the floor of the shed and grabbed a length of live electric fencing. It was desperate and crazy, but in that moment it was all he could think of. He thought maybe he could zap his boy back to life, as though the live wire was some kind of makeshift defibrillator. He was panicking and crying and begging Stephen to come back but it was hopeless. The electric current did nothing and our boy was gone.

I can't imagine what was going through Dad's mind as he carried Stephen back across the farm to Mum. It haunts me when I think about it even now. How could they survive the death of a third child? Dad laid my little brother gently down on the back lawn and ran into the house yelling for Mum, who was still in bed asleep. 'You've got to come, you've got to come quick!'

What awaited her — and my eleven-year-old sister who was also woken by the screaming — was worse than anything she had dared fear. The son she loved so deeply and fiercely was lying dead on the patch of grass where Lance's funeral had taken place sixteen years before.

Mum took in the scene, her boy lying dead on the wet grass, and she could not accept what she saw. She ran inside and called an ambulance, crying and shouting, 'Send help, please send help!'

The operator had difficulty understanding what she was saying. Then Mum said 'Don't worry, it's hopeless, he's dead', and threw the phone down before running back outside. She was angry now because Stephen was covered in mud and cow shit, which he would have hated. For a country boy, he had a surprisingly low tolerance for dirt.

Suddenly she was up again and running. She ran in her nightie the 300 metres to my grandparents' house, across a paddock in bare feet and over a little footbridge. 'Stephen's dead!' she screamed, before turning on her heels and running back. She didn't know what to do; her son had died and it was the end of the world.

In their stunned state my parents eventually carried Stephen inside, changed him out of his dirty clothes and laid him on his bed. It was important to Mum to make him comfortable and safe and warm. The ambulance arrived, but obviously there was nothing they could do. The police turned up and asked some questions, because that's what happens after a sudden death. Then everyone was gone and it was just Mum and Dad, my sister and their dead son, who right now should have been loading his golf clubs into the car and heading off with Dad.

They knew they had to tell me what had happened. Mum managed to track down the cellphone number of my team manager, Jackie, and somehow found the courage to dial it. She calmly explained what had happened and asked to speak to me in a quiet area. Jackie took me into a side room at Christchurch airport and handed me the phone.

'Toni, it's Mum. Stephen's had an accident.'

At first I thought he must've broken his leg, or maybe even his neck. He had been given a motorbike for Christmas and in my mind I was already cursing the thing.

'Is he okay? How bad is it?'

'It's bad, Tones. He's died.'

The next few hours are a blur. I remember walking out of that little room and staring blankly at my teammates, who realised something bad must have happened. A couple of the girls were from Taranaki and knew Stephen and they tried their best to comfort me, but I felt an overwhelming sense of claustrophobia. I needed to get out of there — everything suddenly felt very foreign and unfamiliar.

My manager went into overdrive to get me on the next flight home. She came with me and my older cousin Brad who was coincidentally on the same flight. He took on the job of looking after me, sitting next to me and probably trying to work out what the hell you say to an eighteen-year-old whose life has just been torn apart.

The weird thing is that from the outside I probably seemed calm. A deep state of shock was setting in and it felt as if I was dissociated from my body. I don't think I cried. The reality was too horrible to accept. It simply could not be true that my little brother would not be there when I got home. He was such a vital and special part of our family; it wouldn't work without him.

I'll never forget that walk off the plane and across the tarmac in New Plymouth that day. It was like I could feel the years of grief and anguish that lay ahead, weighing me down with every step I took towards my devastated family.

We drove home in a stunned silence. I knew those roads like the back of my hand, but the view wasn't the same anymore: everything seemed different. I walked down the hallway straight to Stephen's bedroom. There was no escaping it now. There he was. my brother tucked into his bed looking almost exactly the same as before but also completely, horrifyingly different.

Some people draw comfort from seeing their loved ones after they've passed away, but not me — I didn't like it at all. That was not my brother in that bed. The Stephen I knew and loved was gone and in his place was a lifeless body. Every part of me ached for my little brother.

Word spread quickly and the house began to fill with people. In our little pocket of the world families put down roots and don't move, so these were people who had known my parents forever. The ties ran deep. They had been there when Lance died and when Tracy died, and they were here now, with a shared sense of utter disbelief that it could have happened again. Every single person who walked into our house was in a state of shock. But they swooped in, wrapped us up in love and support, and between them made sure we were not alone in those first few days.

Eight cups of tea a day is normal in a farming house, but this was more like twenty. I can still hear the kettle boiling, the clinking of the cups, teaspoons stirring and the dishwasher being constantly loaded and unloaded. We had to talk to everyone who came through the door and it was exhausting, but I was so grateful for the busyness of the house because that is probably what kept us from falling apart. We talked, we passed around the biscuits, we made another pot of tea. It all helped to distract us from the hideous truth that our fourteen-year-old Stephen, the darling of our family, lay dead in the bedroom down the hall.

I was so relieved that it wasn't left to Kirsty and me to hold our parents together. We were young and struggling with our own emotions, let alone coping with Mum's and Dad's. I genuinely remember thinking 'I'm so glad you came' about every person who turned up at our front door during that period, because they were helping me to help my parents. I didn't want us to be alone.

Most visitors would go to see Stephen in his bedroom. I continued to struggle with it. I felt a cold detachment from him in that state — I didn't want to see him like that. It broke my heart, and I remember feeling really scared of the whole situation. I suppose, looking back, I was in denial. If I acknowledged him in that bedroom properly I was accepting that he was dead. And I hadn't reached that point yet.

Of course I did spend time with him, because a part of me must have known it was important, and now I am pleased I did. It helped me to process that yes, this was real, and no, we weren't getting him back. But now when I close my eyes and remember my brother it's the real Stephen I see. The one who's kicking a rugby ball around on the back lawn or smiling up at me with his cheeky grin. It's the brother who hugged me twice at the airport as I left for my cricket trip, the last time I would ever see him.

My grief seemed bottomless. There were times I cried so hard I couldn't breathe. Mum was so strong, with a steely determination that her boy had to be remembered and celebrated properly. She put together a big photo board filled with pictures of Stephen taken throughout his life. The day before his funeral I stood in front of that board, taking in every single image of the precious boy I felt so lucky to have called my brother. Suddenly the horror of how much we had lost overwhelmed me. Mum found me sobbing and gasping for breath on the floor.

I now realise it was a panic attack. My feelings in that moment were so intense I thought I was going to die of sadness. How Mum managed to hold it together seeing me in that state I don't know, because she must have wanted to join me in a heap on the floor. But she gave me a paper bag to breathe into and comforted me as I sobbed.

As a family we lived in a kind of no-man's-land in those first days after Stephen's death. We were just drowning in sadness. Mum was adamant the funeral should happen soon, knowing from past experience that delaying it only prolonged the pain. She and Dad were grateful when a family friend, Simon Ball, stepped in and told them he would organise the funeral. They could leave it all to him. Mum and Dad chose the music and the readings and venue, then this wonderful friend dealt with all the logistics.

One thing my parents have learnt through their losses is to

accept help. People care so much in the aftermath of a tragedy and they *want* to help. We were surrounded by the love of our little community. A good friend, John Lucas, took over the running of the farm which was a godsend, and allowed my dad time to grieve. Someone even snuck over in the early hours of the morning before the funeral and polished our car so it was gleaming. You don't forget those things.

Almost a thousand people came to Stephen's send-off, packing out the New Plymouth Boys' High School hall. They came and they wept with us, and every single person there showed us just how loved Stephen was and how much they cared about our family. Mum had firm ideas about how the day should be: it was a celebration of her boy, and she didn't want any of us wearing black. 'That's what you wear when old people die,' she said. I don't remember what I wore but it definitely wasn't black. My memories of the day are strangely patchy; I think it's because I was traumatised.

I remember thinking beforehand that no way would I be able to get through the funeral, but I managed to pull myself together. I wish now I had been strong enough to make a speech, because there was so much I would love to have told everyone about Stephen and what he meant to me. But I just couldn't. Instead, I read a poem.

Mum, on the other hand, was extraordinary. She did us proud, standing up in front of all those people and talking so beautifully about her son. She wanted every person in that hall to know how awesome Stephen was, how cheeky and funny he was, how he loved the farm and his rugby, and how he was growing into a thoughtful, kind and hardworking young man who made us all so bloody proud.

I honestly don't know how she did it, but I'll always remember her standing up there beside her son's coffin, promising him he would never be forgotten. There wasn't a dry eye in the school hall that day. Stephen's classmates were there; his surf club and rugby friends; all their parents and siblings; his teachers from primary, intermediate and now Boys' High. He was only fourteen, but he had obviously touched a lot of people.

Mum insisted we play all Stephen's favourite music, including the classic 'Who Let the Dogs Out?' It wasn't your typical funeral song, but it was really good because it gave everyone a bit of a laugh. Stephen loved Savage Garden so we played 'I Knew I Loved You', then 'Tears in Heaven' and 'Stand by Me' as we said our final goodbyes. At the end, as Stephen's coffin was carried out of the hall, the Boys' High students, all 1200 of them, performed the most spine-tingling haka I've ever witnessed. It was unforgettable.

After the funeral I was hit with a crashing sense of 'what now?'. I had to reimagine my life without my brother in it and I didn't know where to start. I didn't have any desire to do anything. For the first time my future felt scary and I wondered if any of us would ever feel happiness again. It didn't seem remotely possible. I also felt a heavy responsibility as the eldest child to support my parents in any way I could.

That's when I came to realise the importance of friends and family. I want to say to anyone who has a friend or neighbour who has suffered a tragedy: just turn up. It doesn't matter if you don't know what to say or how to act, it will be such a comfort having you there, knowing you care. Sophie was a wonderful support around that time, my boyfriend Rhys was great, too, and my parents' friends continued their daily visits. Every time we opened the front door someone had delivered yet another meal or more baking, and Dad's mates helped to keep the farm ticking over.

There wasn't anything anyone could do to make us feel less sad, but being wrapped up in kindness and love probably kept us all from falling off an emotional cliff. Mum and Dad still talk about their friend Darryl Edwards, who turned up every evening without fail to sit with them. Sometimes they talked about Stephen and their grief, sometimes they talked about the farm or the weather, and other times they sat in silence. But every night they heard his little Toyota MR2 coming up the driveway, and in the darkest times it reminded them they weren't alone. Darryl's visits continued for at least a year.

A bout a week after Stephen's accident my parents realised we had not left the house except to attend the funeral. 'We need some air,' said Dad, and he bundled Mum, Kirsty and me into the car for a drive to the beach for ice-cream.

It was a beautiful summer's day and I remember looking out the car window at all the people smiling and chatting and happy. I know a lot of people have this experience after they lose someone close to them, but I was shocked. This seemed so wrong — how could they be acting normally, as if nothing had happened? Our lives had been blown apart, yet the world was still spinning, people were still enjoying their summer. Everything looked different to me now: the beach, the local shops, even our house. It was at this moment that I knew things were never going to be the same for any of us.

Looking back, I realise it's a vital part of the grieving process to be reminded that life carries on. You can't simply stop; it's a matter of putting one foot in front of the other on a scary new path. In the beginning, though, that didn't seem right. I had no idea how I could survive the pain, or this new life without my little brother.

That first outing turned out to be fairly disastrous. We had pulled up to a dairy close to our local favourite beach, and as we were getting out of the car we saw two girls racing each other on motorised scooters. The one in front turned to look at her friend and didn't notice a pedestrian crossing ahead.

She went straight through it, collecting a woman and her two small children on the way. I can still see the image of this little three-year-old thrown up into the air like a rag doll.

There were bodies strewn down the road and someone was screaming. Dad and I sprinted towards them while Mum called an ambulance. The young girl was unconscious, her mother was screaming because she thought she was dead, and it was all hideously triggering, considering what we had just been through. Dad was about to start CPR on the little girl, just as he had done with Stephen, when she regained consciousness.

It wasn't what we needed, and poor Dad — it was less than a week since he had held his own child lifeless in his arms. We drove home from that beach trip all a little bruised and shocked, and it would be a while before we were brave enough to attempt another outing.

Broken

You grieve for so many different reasons when you lose someone close to you. A big part of Mum's sadness was knowing that Kirsty and I would now always carry the pain and grief she knew so well. Every mother wants to protect their children and it devastated

Mum that she couldn't protect Stephen from what happened, or us girls from losing him. She could help us through it, but she couldn't stop our pain no matter how hard she tried.

The grief knocked us all in different ways. I struggled for a long time with guilt. I felt guilty for being alive when Stephen had been taken from us, and I was conflicted about how you were meant to carry on after losing someone you loved so much. Was it okay to have moments of joy? It definitely didn't feel right when I caught myself laughing or having fun. I'd think 'How can I be happy when Stephen is dead?'

There were days when I felt like I couldn't win. I didn't want to be sad anymore, but I didn't want to be happy either in case that meant I was forgetting Stephen. It was all very confusing and I know Kirsty felt the same. Mum knew exactly how we were feeling and it was not what she wanted for us. She was determined we would laugh and have fun with our friends, but this was easier said than done. The guilt was ever-present. On several occasions I remember faking being happy to not add to the burden Mum was already carrying.

Mum was broken-hearted, but she did an incredible job of hiding it from us. I would watch her going about her day, cooking dinner or taking us places, and I would think 'How are you surviving this?' But I was old enough to know that her brave face was for our benefit. I heard her sobs through her bedroom door at night, and I heard the anguished arguments between her and Dad. There was a lot going on and I became determined to work out what I could do to make things easier for both of them. In those initial weeks after Stephen died I vowed that for the rest of my life I would do everything I could to make Mum and Dad happy. I would never, ever do anything that might make their lives harder.

That sense of responsibility has never left me, in fact, it became one of the drivers of my life — to be the best possible daughter for my parents, who so deserve happiness. I knew it was up to me (and Kirst, but she was still young) to bring joy back into their lives and to somehow redress the imbalance. Every success I've had — in my career and my family life — has been as much for them as for me. They deserve all the highs they can get.

Grief, though, is a long and complicated journey, and my parents' familiarity with the road ahead didn't make it any easier this time around. The first few months were bleak. All the sadness and loss that had been pushed to the side since Lance, Tracy and Nana died came back to hit Mum with force. She got up every morning, put on her brave face and tried to maintain the usual routine for our sake, but not a day went by when she didn't cry. She was consumed by grief in all its guises — disbelief, misery, anger, numbness. There was such a colossal sense of emptiness.

Dad's way of coping was to plunge into farm life to distract himself from the pain. He refused to let guilt be part of his grieving for Stephen, but Mum struggled with that at times

— she was angry that Stephen was on the quadbike at all, let alone without a helmet. She hated us kids riding that thing, but the reality is that every single one of us country kids rode around on quadbikes, and Dad trusted that we were sensible enough to handle it. He saw Stephen's fall for what it was: a terrible, terrible accident.

Geoff Street is a pragmatic man; he knew there was zero point carrying guilt around. Mum took out a lot of her anger on him, but he remained as steady as a rock. 'We've just got to get on with things. If I go down we'll all go down,' I remember him saying. He was determined not to crack, but I expect that meant he bottled up an awful lot of his feelings after Stephen's death.

Mum was haunted by Stephen's final moments and whether he had suffered. A post-mortem found the cause of death was asphyxiation from the weight of the bike, so a helmet probably wouldn't have helped him anyway. The hope is that he was knocked unconscious straight away and had no knowledge of what was happening. There was no indication that he had struggled, so we all held onto the hope his death happened quickly, without fear or pain. We chose to believe he didn't suffer, because the alternative was unbearable.

Mum began winding herself in knots about the things she wished she had done to make Stephen's life happier, which upset me because he had a wonderful childhood. There is nothing Mum could have done to be a better mother, and

Stephen loved her with all his heart. But she still kicks herself for not taking him to our uncle's bach in the Coromandel that summer. Whangamata was his favourite place, and he had been begging Mum to take him and his best mate there for a weekend during the school holidays. Mum now wished she had made it a priority, like buying the John Britten book.

I hope she also remembers the many, many amazing things she and Dad did to make Stephen's life special. They took him to All Blacks games; we had an incredible family holiday on the Gold Coast; and for Christmas he got the two-wheeler motorbike he had been wanting for years. But most of all they gave him unconditional love for his whole fourteen years. He was a happy and fulfilled boy who had all he needed, and I'm sure now Mum knows and can be comforted by that.

I felt I couldn't possibly go away to Lincoln. How could I walk out on Mum, Dad and Kirsty now? I would be lying if I said I didn't want to escape from it all, but I felt I needed to stay to make sure they were okay.

My parents were torn. They didn't want Stephen's death to ruin my future, but they also didn't know whether it was sensible for me to go away with the grief so fresh. They agonised over it, but in the end they decided I should give it a go. 'If you hate it or you're not coping you can come home,' Mum said.

I was relieved the decision was made for me, and packing up and getting organised for my new life became an important distraction for all of us. We promised to talk every day, and I made Mum, Dad and Kirsty swear they would tell me if they needed me to come home. I felt as if I was abandoning them, and I was especially worried about my sister, who was only eleven. She had only known life with me and Stephen in it, and she had just lost him. Now I was about to walk out of her life, too. The busy household was about to feel very empty.

Kirsty slept in our parents' bed for the first few months after Stephen died. Then they dragged her mattress into their room and it stayed there for the rest of the year. It helped her, but it also helped Mum and Dad, who wanted to keep her close.

Before I left, Mum gave me a scrapbook and urged me to write down my feelings about Stephen. I guess she was worried I would go down there and bottle everything up, which is exactly what I did. But the scrapbook became a vital part of my recovery — in fact I wrote in that book sporadically for ten years. Sometimes it was just one line — *Missing Stephen today*; other times I would write for hours, pages and pages of words trying to figure it all out. How would our family ever get over this and learn to be happy again?

I'm so thankful Mum encouraged me to write things down, because it became an outlet for my sadness and anger and the overwhelming mix of feelings that comes with losing someone you love. I still flick through it sometimes and it's like watching an old home movie. The memories come flooding back and it makes me realise how far we have all come. We survived.

Back then, none of us were sure we would.

First kiss

When I first arrived at Lincoln University I was a bit of a mess. On the face of it I put on a great show, and most people probably thought I was coping brilliantly. I realise now, though, that I was in total denial. My brother had died five weeks earlier and there I was, 800 kilometres from home and the only people who truly knew what I was going through.

First-year students lived in halls of residence. My new home was called, unbelievably, Stevens Hall. On a positive day I guess you could say it was comforting, but the name of my new home also served as a daily reminder of my loss.

Stevens Hall was made up of three three-storey 1970s buildings that housed about sixty students like me, all taking our nervous first steps towards adult life. Except they weren't like me, because even though I'm sure everyone had their own stuff going on, at the time I felt like I was the only one carrying such fresh baggage.

The anguish of abandoning my family was with me all the time; I missed them heaps and constantly wondered how they were coping, but at the same time was guiltily glad not to be around constant reminders of Stephen's death. Occasionally I cried on the phone to Mum, but, not wanting to add to her sadness, I held a lot back. Thank goodness for Sophie and Mike and Rhys, nearby at Canterbury University. It was a 30-minute drive and it was a trip I made a lot. I was making friends at Lincoln, but I often felt a deep need to be with people from home, who knew my brother and understood the gravity of what had happened.

I could be out at a party, or at the pub having drinks with my mates, when thoughts would creep in, like 'Why are you here? You shouldn't be in this life; you should be at home with your family.' When it all got too much I would find myself in Sophie's little hostel room, sobbing on her bed while she patiently sat with me. It was heavy stuff for two barely eighteen-year-olds, and I'll always be so grateful we decided to study in the same place.

Looking back, I'm still not sure it was the best thing for me to go away so soon. But I went through the motions. I made new friends, went to lectures, partied, played sport and had some great times. I probably seemed no different to all the others, but it was almost as if I had two lives: the one at university, where I got to pretend everything was normal; and the one when I returned home, where the horrifying loss of my brother engulfed me again. They were hard to marry up sometimes.

Slowly I worked out how to navigate my new university life alongside the grief, and most of the time I was okay. Perhaps I was learning how to compartmentalise. Then I would be out one day having fun and — *whoosh* — that familiar pang of grief would hit. How could I be happy when Stephen would never experience happiness again?

I should have been kinder to myself. I know now that grieving for someone doesn't mean you should stop living your life. It doesn't mean you're not allowed to be happy. But it took me quite some time to be okay with that.

Mum and Dad never let on how much they were missing me, but I remember one weekend soon after I arrived I got an awful bout of food poisoning. It got to the point where I was vomiting blood, so I saw a doctor and found out it was *Campylobacter*. Dad couldn't bear the thought of me being so sick on my own in that little room, so he got into his car at midnight, drove through the night to Wellington, slept in the car in the queue for the Cook Strait ferry, then drove halfway down the South Island, arriving at Stevens Hall about lunchtime. That's the kind of person Dad is, and I'm sure getting some time away from the farm would have helped him, too.

When I was first offered a cricket scholarship to Lincoln I remember thinking: 'This is a really random choice for me, but at least I'm from a farm, and Lincoln is where farm kids go. I'll fit in nicely.' But I quickly discovered that my fellow students were a totally different type of rural type from those I knew. The Taranaki dairy farmers I'd grown up with pretty much wore rugby shorts or overalls. They were rough and ready; they pulled on anything that was comfy. But these kids from Canterbury beef and sheep farms were different. They wore a daily uniform of cream-coloured moleskins and Aertex shirts with the collars turned up. The girls wore strings of pearls, which were not big in rural Taranaki.

A couple of weeks in, I was sitting around in the common room with Karla, a friend from home who was at Lincoln on a netball scholarship, when we spotted a pair of boys we quite liked the look of. One was tall and blond, the other dark-haired and stocky with broad shoulders. They were good-looking, but mainly they stood out for us because they looked like the kind of boys we knew from home. Karla's eyes lit up. 'Look, they're not wearing moleskins!' she whispered. 'They're definitely the hottest guys in first-year. I like the tall one; you can have the other one.'

Although I didn't know it at the time, 'the other one' was Matt France, a shy, sporty boy from Timaru who would turn out to be the best thing that's ever happened to me.

I still had my high-school boyfriend, Rhys, down the road at design school in Christchurch, though, so I didn't give these guys much thought. However, it transpired that one of Matt's best mates lived in the room next door to mine, and before long we became friends. Matt would visit his friend Hadyn, and pop in to say hello to me. Over time the visits to his friend became briefer and briefer, until the point where he was spending most of his spare time hanging out with me.

From the moment I met him I could tell he was different from the other guys. He wasn't as confident as many of the other first-years, who were full of bravado, having shaken off the constraints of home. Matt had a calmness to him. He had a baby face but he seemed older, more mature than most of the other boys.

We were struck by how much we had in common. Like

me, he was at Lincoln to play sport, and was very focused on his rugby career. And, like me, he was living with grief, having lost his dad, Steve, when he was fourteen. Yep, his dad was called Steve. Who knows what it meant, but the frequency with which that name kept popping up in my life was becoming a little weird.

Teenage boys are not known for their willingness to discuss emotional issues, so Matt — who had boarded at Otago Boys' High School before Lincoln — had kept his feelings very much to himself in the years since his father's death. It wasn't until I gave him a lift home from rugby practice one night that he opened up. As we sat talking in my parked car the floodgates finally opened. We talked for hours.

I can't explain how powerful it was to find someone else who had experienced the pain I had been going through, and who understood the confusing reality of living with grief. We bonded over our mutual crushing acceptance that your family can never be the same again, and the weird guilt that comes with compartmentalising the experience. Until then, I had felt so alone with those feelings.

Matt's dad, Steve, had been battling cancer for years, but even though they all knew death was a possibility, it was as horrible and shocking as if they did not. He was only 42, and Matt missed him so badly. He felt cheated out of a father in the same way that I felt cheated out of a brother. For an eighteen-year-old boy, Matt talked about all this with such clarity and bravery and emotional depth. And yet this was the first time he had talked to anyone about it in the four years since his father died. I was so impressed with him. He had so much substance.

After that our connection was sealed and we became the firmest of friends. Matt was studying environmental science, but sport was his big dream, as it was for me. We loved campus life at Lincoln, but it was my cricket and netball, and his rugby, that took most of our focus.

I should point out here that by the middle of first year my relationship with Rhys had run its course. We had totally different lives now and it was time to go our separate ways. It didn't have anything to do with Matt on a conscious level; I honestly only looked on him as a friend at this point. We were part of a tight group of about six mates at Lincoln who spent all our spare time together. If I hadn't seen Matt on a given day I'd seek him out, and in the holidays, when I went home to New Plymouth, I missed him so much we would spend ages on the phone each night.

I'm not sure why it took us so long to get together, because to our friends it was pretty clear it was only a matter of time. I had certainly thought a lot about the prospect but I didn't want to jeopardise our friendship. Matt was adorably candid about his feelings for me; from fairly early on he made it clear he wanted our relationship to be more. It was me who was holding out.

On the face of it, Matt was a bit of a rugby-head, but I quickly discovered his intellectual side and we bonded over our love of robust conversation. We debated constantly, and he drove me crazy because he would pick a standpoint on something just to annoy me. Then he would never back down. His outspoken disdain for pop music, which I loved, is a good example.

'You only like it because everyone else does,' he'd say. 'It has no musical merit whatsoever. It's rubbish.'

'That's not true!' I'd scream. 'You have to actually *listen* to a song before you decide you hate it. You're just trying to be cool.'

He would have been a great debater if he had wanted to be. When I started out in journalism he was so helpful to me: I'd run things past him for another perspective, which was always well thought through and from an empathic angle. He's one of the most sensitive and emotionally switched-on people I've ever known.

One night, when a bunch of us were hanging out having a few drinks, Mum called. Matt, his customary shyness obviously banished by the beer, grabbed my phone off me. 'I'm going to marry your daughter one day!' he yelled down the phone, before chucking it back to me. Goodness knows what Mum thought, but I found it hilarious.

It wasn't until the following year, when we had both moved into student flats in Christchurch, that Matt and I finally got together. It was the night of his nineteenth birthday. He and his mates had a big party at their place and we all ended up going out afterwards to a karaoke bar in town. I don't know how it happened, but it was there, in a dark, noisy karaoke booth with all our mates around us, that we first kissed. No one was remotely surprised.

From that first kiss, I knew Matt was going to be a special person in my life.

One of the nicest things about being with him was the way he made me feel. I was never in any doubt that he loved me and that I could trust him. Every day things just got better and better between us. For a teenage boy he was quite extraordinary in his ability to show his feelings. I loved him, and I felt loved by him, and that was exactly what I needed. I didn't have the emotional energy to engage in a difficult relationship, which is why I felt so grateful to Matt for how easy it was to be together. No arguments, no emotional manipulation or game-playing — we were a couple and that was that.

We didn't rush things, though. I flatted with a bunch of girls, including Sophie, and Matt lived down the road with six guys. We would watch each other's sport at the weekends and get together at night to do what students do — drink too much and have fun.

I travelled home every long weekend and university holiday. I was always happy to get back to the farm, but the pain of opening the front door to find Stephen gone never diminished. The house didn't feel right without him, and his loss continued to hang heavily in the air.

We tried our best, but our first Christmas without Stephen was pretty miserable. Mum put up a tree and a few decorations and cooked a turkey, but we probably should all have just stayed in bed because none of us wanted to celebrate. What was there to celebrate without Stephen? On 'happy' occasions like this, Kirsty and I knew it was up to us to lift spirits. We honestly tried to pretend we were having fun, but I know we all agree now it was terrible.

None of us knew how we were supposed to act, which made it very awkward.

When people hear about grief or losing someone they think about sadness and loss, but they don't perhaps realise it permeates everything. It's hard to describe, but you are left with moments when you don't know how you're meant to be anymore. The naturalness of the life you knew has been ripped away, and just existing — and co-existing with others who are left — takes effort. It's like learning to walk again.

Toni Street,
One News

W hen I was little, if someone asked what I wanted to be when I grew up, I'd say 'A singer or a Silver Fern.' Being raised in a sport-obsessed family it felt totally normal to set my sights on representing New Zealand, and, after realising my singing ability probably wasn't going to take me to Hollywood or Broadway, I doubled down on making it to the top in netball and/or cricket.

But I also remember, at about the age of ten, becoming fascinated by the sports reporters on TV. Watching the 6 p.m. news was a big part of our family routine, so stars like April Ieremia and Bernadine Oliver-Kerby were household names and I thought they had the best job in the world. Imagine travelling around to all the top sports games, and then going on TV to tell everyone about it! Mum took me to a netball game in New Plymouth once where Bernadine was hosting, and I clearly remember thinking 'That there is my dream job.'

I briefly considered applying for broadcasting school when I left school, but I knew how hard it was to get in and I suppose I had a bit of a wobble in confidence. So when I was offered the scholarship at Lincoln it was an easy decision. I mean it's not every day someone offers to pay your university fees, plus it gave me access to the High Performance Centre, where I knew I would be training with some of the best cricketers and coaches in the country.

Most of the degrees offered at Lincoln were horticulture- and farming-focused, which I knew wasn't for me, so I enrolled in a commerce degree, majoring in marketing and management. I had done well enough at accounting at school, so it seemed like a sensible choice. I was realistic enough to know I needed a backup plan in case my sporting career didn't work out.

I'm a girly swot, so I worked hard at university and ended up getting my degree with pretty good marks. When I was asked to stay on and do an Honours year I was tempted, but Mum said to me, 'You've got your degree. If you're ever going to give this broadcasting thing a crack, it should be now.'

She hadn't forgotten my childhood dream of sports reporting, and always believed I could do it. So we researched the options for journalism study in New Zealand and discovered there was a one-year postgraduate diploma course at Canterbury University, which covered print, radio and television. It was run by Jim Tully, a legend in journalism circles, and entry was restricted to twenty people a year.

This, I told Mum, was the place for me. Just reading the course information got me excited. I decided I would give the application my all, and if I didn't get in, I'd go back to Lincoln and do the Honours year.

To give myself the best possible chance of being selected, I started writing sports reports for the Lincoln University magazine, and I did some work experience at *The Press* in Christchurch and the *Taranaki Daily News*. It all looked good on my CV.

I was equally stoked and terrified when I made the shortlist for the course and travelled to Wellington for a face-to-face interview with Jim Tully and some of the other lecturers. I didn't pretend to know a lot about journalism, but I guess my wide-eyed enthusiasm convinced them I'd give it my best shot, because a few days later I got the call. I was part of the 2006 intake.

Making the cut was the confidence boost I needed and I was so happy, but at the same time I was more than a little daunted. I had been warned it would be a tough and intense year, with a significant workload.

But I walked in on my first day, looked around at the nineteen others all as nervous and excited as me, and I just knew I had found my thing.

Journalism, we were told on day one, was about storytelling. There were stories everywhere; we just had to know how to look for them and it was all about finding an angle. Jim's experience and passion for the craft ignited something in all of us. We felt we were part of something special, and to be honest I still feel that every time I head to work. Jim delighted us with tales from his years of working in newsrooms, and he taught us there was always more to a story than first met the eye. We were encouraged to dig a little deeper and always go one step further — out of our comfort zones.

Above all, though — and this is what made Jim special — we were taught to be kind, and to treat everyone we came across with respect and compassion. 'Be nice to the little people,' he said, reminding us we could be hungry and ambitious without being arseholes. It was a lesson I never forgot.

Every day I couldn't wait to get to class. It was like fuel to the fire and I couldn't wait to experience the thrill of real-life reporting. I wouldn't have to wait long because work experience was a big component of the diploma and we were expected to be out there looking for stories right from the very start. We learnt about court reporting, police reporting, general news gathering, how to write for newspapers, and how to create scripts and voicers for TV and radio. We were schooled on media law and ethics, subediting, and had daily teeline shorthand lessons. I loved every single bit of it. There was genuinely no part of that year that I found boring or uninteresting, even if passing the teeline requirements was a little stressful! I knew without an ounce of hesitation that I had landed where I wanted to be. This was me.

There was a real sense of camaraderie in that course, with the twenty of us spending every day together in the journalism wing at Canterbury University, and I made some firm friends there. One of my biggest allies was Anna Leask, now one of *The New Zealand Herald*'s senior reporters. But there was also an undercurrent of competition, because we all knew our career paths depended on how well we did and it was a fight to see who would land the six-month internships offered by several media outlets at the end of the course. I was determined to be one of the best in the class so that I would get one. I didn't know where it would be, but my dream of being a TV sports reporter was still bubbling away.

It wasn't long into my studies that it became clear I couldn't seriously pursue a journalism career while still aiming to be a top-level sportsperson. Something had to give. I was still playing rep netball for Canterbury and cricket for Central Districts, but since discovering journalism my priorities had flipped. Sport was now secondary. It was a weird realisation, because sport had always been such a huge part of my life, but I knew my dream of becoming a Silver Fern or a White Fern was over. I walked away with no regrets, safe in the knowledge that those years in a team environment had set me up well. Discipline, hard work, focus and the importance of teamwork were well ingrained, and they were to come in handy in my career.

My sport was scaling back, but Matt's rugby career was going from strength to strength. He was playing for the New Zealand Under-19 team while finishing off his degree, and much to our excitement he had been selected for the Crusaders Academy. We were still living in separate flats but very much a couple.

I was also discovering just how romantic my boyfriend was — far more than me! He would buy me little gifts and write me poems. Early in our relationship, Matt travelled to Paris for the Under-19 Rugby World Cup. It was a huge deal and I was incredibly proud of him. He was away for six weeks and I wasn't expecting to hear from him much because I knew he would be busy training, travelling, playing and having an amazing time.

But every single day he managed to call me from wherever he was staying. He sent me love letters, and when he got home he gave me a beautiful silver bracelet. I was so touched because I knew he was completely broke. He was struggling to even pay his uni fees, so to know he had put aside some money for a gift was so lovely.

Now, after twelve years of marriage, he's still a romantic. I'll often come home to find he's sent me flowers just to say 'I love you', or because he knows I've had a full-on week. I try to do nice things in return, but I know he would agree I'm nowhere near as mushy as he is.

Probably because of the way we had first bonded over our grief, our relationship had a depth that was a bit unusual for a pair of teenagers. We relied on each other a lot, and it was hugely comforting that neither of us felt we had to keep our feelings to ourselves when those waves of sadness came calling. Life was good, but that invisible cloak had settled firmly on my shoulders and I was still getting used to it.

As every journalist knows, you never forget your first big scoop, and mine happened while I was still a student. I'd love to say it was my journalistic brilliance that led to a full-page story in the *Sunday Star-Times* newspaper, but there was a decent sprinkling of luck involved. My flatmate played hockey with Honor Dillon, a member of the Black Sticks who was making jewellery on the side and doing pretty well from it. I thought it would make an interesting story. Bubbling away in the back of my mind was the fact that she was dating an All Black, and not just any All Black — it was Dan Carter. If I could get Honor talking about her jewellery *and him*, well, that would definitely help my chances of getting the story published.

I plucked up the courage to ask her for an interview and she agreed. We talked about all sorts of things, including her relationship. I typed it up and, with Jim's encouragement, offered it to the *Sunday Star-Times* news desk. I didn't have high hopes but it was worth a shot.

You can imagine the thrill when an email came back saying they would like to publish it and offering me $300. It was my first byline and I would be paid! I was so happy. I now had my first published story to add to my CV. I couldn't believe it!

My next big story was splashed on the front page of *The Timaru Herald*, where half our class was doing work experience while the other half worked at the *Marlborough Express* in Blenheim.

We arrived in the small town, introduced ourselves to the newsroom staff and hit the ground searching for stories. The reporters there must have been rolling their eyes at us bright-eyed, bushy-tailed students ambushing their town, but nothing could dampen our enthusiasm. It felt so exciting to finally get to do the real thing and I was determined to hunt down a decent yarn or two.

I can't remember how, but I came across a guy who was trying to recruit people for the Middlemarch Singles Ball, an event designed to help southern farmers find partners. It wasn't the first one but it seemed to be gaining in popularity so I managed to find an angle and get a story out of it. It wasn't hard, because the ball was a brilliant concept and the organiser was such a charismatic man. He gave me great quotes, and I was so happy when the editor put it on the front page. I still have that clipping somewhere.

Another story I was proud of that year was a TV project, where we had to choose an issue or a story and put together a piece suitable for something like the six o'clock news. I decided to focus on over-hydration, because Sophie had recently collapsed during a half-marathon after drinking too much water. I thought it was an issue worth shining a light on because most athletes are worried about the opposite problem, dehydration. I interviewed Sophie about her experience and some experts on the phenomenon, too, working away on the three-minute piece over several months.

When I landed one of the *One News* internships at the end of my course (one of the best things that's ever happened to me), I showed the clip to Mark Hannan, head of the TVNZ news team at the time, and he liked it. He asked me to reshoot the story for them and it could go to air. I was *so* stoked because I had expected it would be weeks or even months before I got to do my own story. So I reshot it, interviewed Sophie again, and rewrote the script.

I was too inexperienced to voice the story myself, so Ruwani Perera, an experienced TVNZ reporter, did it for me, and the story made it to air. Ru felt bad that I wasn't voicing my own story, but I wasn't even slightly miffed. 'Are you kidding me? I've only been here a few weeks!' I said. I was just happy she felt comfortable enough voicing the script of such a novice.

I was hired as an intern at *One News* in Auckland on an annual salary of $26,000 ($13,000 for the six months), which was barely enough to live on, but I didn't care. Getting to work in the country's best television newsroom was everything I had ever dreamed of. I just lived on spaghetti on toast. Even if I had wanted to spend money on nice dinners out, I was usually working, so that solved that.

I had also been offered an internship at Radio Sport, which was appealing because it was sport and I loved the people who worked there, but I knew that turning down an internship at TVNZ would have been foolish. I had to opt for the *One News* placement. I would be lying if I said I wasn't super-nervous. Imposter syndrome set in the minute I walked in on that first day and came face to face with the people I had looked up to for years. I looked around and felt totally star-struck — all while pretending to be totally cool about it of course.

Judy Bailey had just left, so Wendy Petrie was the 6 p.m. newsreader with Simon Dallow. I remember being particularly star-struck by Peter Williams because I had watched his cricket commentary and sports coverage of the Olympics for years, and there he was, right in front of me.

Everyone seemed so talented and so professional and I felt quite overwhelmed to be among them. On my first day I was sent out with a reporter called Hadyn Jones, who turned out to be married to a Taranaki girl I went to school with, so immediately I felt more at ease. As I sit and write this I've just finished two fill-in shifts hosting *Seven Sharp* with Hadyn, which would have seemed completely unbelievable back then.

Most of my time on the internship was spent accompanying other reporters to stories, which was the best way to learn. I did my first 'death knock', where you turn up on someone's doorstep in the hope that the person might be happy to talk to you about their loved one who has recently died. It's terrifying. Intrusive, awkward, heartbreaking, and it never sat well with me. But I like to think my own life experience gave me the right tools for these situations. If the person didn't want you there, you left. No pushing back, no negotiating.

I quickly learnt the privilege of this position: being welcomed into the home of a grieving family to talk about and honour their loved one is a very special role to be entrusted with. Even now when I'm interviewing people I am always conscious of the fact that they're opening themselves up and being vulnerable, so they must be treated with respect

I absorbed every single aspect of how the newsroom worked. I watched the way the reporters conducted their interviews, how they treated their subjects. I studied their scripts and tried to mimic the way they spoke and held themselves in front of the camera. I cringe now when I watch my tapes from those early days. I think all new reporters do it, but I seem to be trying to act like a seasoned TV journalist with a very serious stare and a grown-up voice. I remember trying to make my voice much deeper than it naturally was. 'Toni Street, *One News*.' I used to practise that in the mirror. I guess I was trying to sound professional and experienced, because I didn't yet have the confidence to just be myself. Pretty cringe when I think about it now!

My first live cross, where you're beamed into the studio, was for the midday news, which is where juniors start before being set loose in the prime-time 6 p.m. spot. It was an interview with Sir Peter Leitch (aka the Mad Butcher) at Mt Smart Stadium and I was terrified. If something goes wrong in a live cross, like you stumble your words or freeze up, there's no hiding. You just have to salvage what you can and try not to make a complete idiot of yourself. I couldn't have had a better interviewee for my first ever live — Sir Peter expertly guided the interview and did most of the talking. I hardly had to say a thing. Sir Peter and I have reminisced about that day many times since; he's such a wonderful man.

I must have been fairly vocal about my passion for sport, because three months into my internship I was moved to the sports desk, and as my internship came to an end I was offered a full-time job.

This was unbelievable. Every day I walked into TVNZ I was literally living my dream.

I was a *One News* sports reporter and I couldn't have been happier.

Growing
pains

Most people can look back and see the point at which
they got their big career break. Mine was about a
year into my time as a sport reporter. I was tapping
away on a script in the newsroom when Barbara Mitchell
appeared. She was the executive producer of TVNZ's netball

coverage, and I overheard her telling someone that one of the netball commentators had fallen ill so she urgently needed someone for an ANZ Championship game the following Saturday. This was Thursday, so she didn't have much time to get it sorted. She looked out across the newsroom and, almost as a joke I think, called out: 'Does anyone here know anything about netball?'

It was one of those moments. I could keep my headphones on, eyes down and say nothing. Or I could pipe up and try to grab this opportunity, for which I knew I was completely and utterly underqualified.

'I do!' I yelled, surprising even myself with my keenness.

'Really?' said Barbara.

'I love netball,' I continued shamelessly. 'I've played it all my life, I'm passionate about it and I'd love to have a crack.'

The next day I was called in for an audition. The producers put an old netball game up on screen and I commentated for about half an hour. I was incredibly nervous, but I knew this was my chance to prove how much I knew about a game I'd been obsessed with since I was about five. I knew all the players and understood the intricacies of the game, so I just went for it.

Barb was obviously happy because she gave me the gig (either that or I was the only option!). At 24, I was pretty green to be commentating, but I had a strong ally in Jenny-May Clarkson (née Coffin). She and I had started at TVNZ the same day, did all our training together and became firm friends.

Commentating was a baptism of fire, but I relished the opportunity and gave it my all.

One of the many learning curves in live television is getting used to comms. In live broadcasting there are two different set-ups: you have either closed comms or open comms. Closed comms is when you receive the occasional message from the director in your earpiece telling you when to throw to an ad break.

But with open comms, which is how it works during live sports broadcasts, you hear absolutely everything the director calls — not only to the presenters but also to the camera operators, the director's assistant and anyone else behind the scenes. In a netball broadcast, for example, there are multiple cameras so your earpiece is constantly receiving information: 'cut to 2,' 'cut to 3', 'go gib', 'close that up on 1' and so on. It's an endless chatter, and you have to learn how to filter it out as you deliver your lines. You have to train yourself to hear the director's voice *only* when it is aimed at you, which could happen at any moment. It was trial by fire. It takes a while to master the skill, I tell you.

When I later had my first presenting shift, reading the sports news on *One News*, everything felt incredibly silent because on the news you have closed comms. I kept thinking the communications were broken!

Presenting netball was a fantastic learning opportunity for me, and prepared me in so many ways for my later hosting jobs. I learnt how to think on my feet, how to fill time when the unexpected occurs, like injuries and delays. Suddenly, with no warning, you have to fill a three-minute gap on live television with relevant, interesting chat. Live sport gives you an excellent grounding that you don't necessarily get in general news.

Another learning curve came courtesy of our sports boss at the time, Chris Mirams. He was an old-school, ex-newspaper journo who did not suffer fools and had exceptionally high expectations. I was terrified of him initially. He would sub-edit your scripts to within an inch of their lives, and if he didn't like what you had written he'd say 'Go back and do it again.'

If you handed in a script that was even one second over the time you had been allocated, it would be sent back with the instruction to redo it. It was a tough environment completely devoid of niceties, which I found pretty stressful at times as a newbie. Every day there was this 6 p.m. deadline to meet — it was immovable and that created a pressure that built through the day.

But I understood what Chris was about — he had a job to do. The flipside was that if your script made it to air unchanged, that was the ultimate compliment. It meant he thought you had done a good job. He would never say so, of course; you just worked it out, and it was the best feeling in the world knowing you'd nailed it. I'm pretty sure that happened to me only once or twice.

There were definitely times when I thought 'Oh boy, this guy is such a hard-arse', but now when I look back I know it gave me the best possible grounding. It was Chris's super-high standards that taught me to script really tightly, and to get to the point of the story without mucking around (even though I may not have appeared exactly grateful at the time).

I remember I was in charge of delivering the Black Caps cricket match report one day, and, as often happened, the game was still in progress as the sports news was going to air. I was in the edit suite and a wicket fell probably three minutes before the sports news was due to start.

I had to make a split-second decision over whether to add to my story to include that fallen wicket or publish the story as I already had it. Because I wanted to impress Chris, I made the call to change it, but I wasn't fast enough and my story missed its slot. So instead of leading the sports news my cricket report got demoted to number two and I remember feeling sick about it. I dragged myself out of the edit booth with my tail between my legs and headed back to the Sports Department expecting a barrelling. But Chris took one look at me and must have realised I was punishing myself enough, because he didn't say a word. I went off to the bathroom for a good cry.

From day one, life as a junior reporter was intense — I don't think I've ever worked so hard. Being the newbie I was often assigned the graveyard shift, from 11 p.m. to 7 a.m., and usually worked weekends. I quickly gained a reputation as someone who always said yes. Another story, an extra shift, a few more hours — it was always a yes from me. I worked my butt off, basically, determined to impress my bosses and prove I wasn't afraid of hard work. But at times I was overwhelmed by it all. We worked so hard all day getting a story to air, then had to do it all again the next day. It was a never-ending pressure-cooker and there were times when I thought 'I can't keep up this pace.'

My first regular live-TV opportunity came when I was asked to do a slot on *Breakfast* every Monday, talking with the hosts, Pippa Wetzell and Paul Henry, about the weekend's sport. I was terrified about joining them on the couch because (a) it was live TV, and (b) it was Paul Henry, who was famous for his unpredictably left-field approach.

Paul could be incredibly entertaining, but I never knew what he was going to ask, and I was always on guard for one of his curve balls. Most of the time I handled it okay — I'd been covering sport all weekend, so I knew who had played where and who had won what. But on one occasion I was talking about tennis and Paul suddenly asked me about lesbians in the tennis world. *Lesbians?* I was completely floored; I didn't know where to go with that or how to respond. I probably went bright red, but somehow I managed to shut it down and move on to the next topic.

Ultimately, those Monday mornings on the *Breakfast* couch with Pippa and Paul were fantastic practice for what was to come. That show had such a great energy, and even though everyone had been up since the crack of dawn there was a real camaraderie and sense of fun. I remember thinking I would love to work on this show, not believing I ever would, because I was a sports reporter.

Matt and I were still together, but we were doing it long distance because he had moved to New Plymouth to play for Taranaki in the National Provincial Championship (NPC). It was a strange time in our relationship and there were several months where we barely saw each other. I was working all the time and Matt was training and playing flat out, so we had to make do with phone calls and texts. Matt even moved in with my parents for three months, which was awesome because when I went home I could see them all in one hit!

It was hard being apart, but I was so busy I didn't have time to dwell on it. I was travelling a lot with my job, mostly around New Zealand covering sports events but also overseas. I went to England to cover the World Netball Series, Singapore for the World Netball Champs, and in 2008 I was part of the reporting team at the Beijing Olympics, which was a trip like no other.

I was living the dream — the whole experience of being a young reporter was such an incredible buzz. I had also learnt to stop trying so hard in front of the camera. I learnt it was okay to be myself and to use my normal voice, which made me feel far more comfortable.

In 2008 Matt was selected for the North Harbour NPC team, which meant we were finally living in the same place again. We found a two-bedroom apartment right in the centre of Auckland and moved in with Sophie and Mike. Mike was working at Fletcher Construction and Soph got a job at TVNZ in the human resources department, so we would skip off to work together in the mornings, and walk home together at night. It was fun. We all worked hard by day, and in the evenings we would converge at home, cook dinner and share a few wines.

Matt and I were secretly a bit gutted when, after a year or so, Sophie and Mike decided to move back to New Plymouth. They got married, and soon after their first child, Isabella, was born, followed a few years later by Theo. They were the first of our friends to have babies and we were so excited for them, but Matt and I were not ready for that step and we missed them. We rented our own place on Auckland's

North Shore so that Matt was closer to his training. We didn't know it at the time, but that first flat ended up being just down the road from the Takapuna home we bought a few years later.

It wasn't long into my TV career that I started to understand the reality of being beamed into Kiwi living rooms each night. People would occasionally recognise me in the street and I loved it when they came up and said hello — it meant they were watching my stories. Friends of Mum and Dad's also started to call and say they'd seen my pieces, and that was often followed by an observation on how I looked — what I was wearing or how I had my hair that night.

Feedback comes in lots of forms, and as my profile grew I started to experience some of the negativity I had been warned about. It never fails to amaze me that there are people out there ready to pounce with a nasty Facebook comment or an unkind email.

I could handle the odd remark about an unflattering dress or a bad hair day, but the criticism ramped up a gear when I became co-host on *Saturday Breakfast* alongside Rawdon Christie in 2013. Breakfast television is like nothing else in the industry. Everything about you is on show for three hours live every day — your personality, your reactions to stories, your opinions, how you hold yourself, the tone you use to make a joke.

This role, with its bigger profile, makes you ripe for the

picking, and no one is immune. It was a huge step up the career ladder, but it became clear not everyone was pleased.

'Please tell Toni to stop smiling so much,' said one viewer in an irate email after my first morning on air.

'Toni laughs too much,' said another. 'She's dizzy.'

I remember calling Mum and asking her to tell me *truthfully* if she thought I was too smiley on air. 'Don't change for anyone,' she said sternly. 'Be yourself. That's what's got you this far so don't change now.' She was absolutely right of course. That turned out to be some of the best advice I've ever had. If people don't like me for who I am, there's not much I can do about that.

But even after fifteen years in broadcasting some of the comments still sting.

One of the worst came in a text message in my first week on The Hits radio station, after I had made the big decision to take on the role of radio breakfast show host while continuing to host *Seven Sharp* in the evening.

'Toni is fat and ugly. She's fake and she's a terrible mum for leaving those poor kids at home and going to work.' Whoa, that one covered all the bases. I had spent weeks agonising over whether working two jobs was the right decision for our family. Matt had quit full time work and was contracting only when it fit.

I tried to brush off that message, but the sting stayed with me for a long time. It felt very personal, and it saddened me to think that someone took the time to write that and send it. Do these people think we're not human and these things don't hurt?

My way of dealing with the trolls has always been to tell myself they must have their own issues going on in their lives. The impulse to be so mean to someone you've never met is baffling to me. I try to ignore it, but I can't help thinking 'I'm a good person — why would you be so feral?'

I have definitely hardened up over the years, but I remain a sensitive and emotional person and I wouldn't want to end up numbed to this stuff.

A lot of the 'feedback' is levelled at my appearance, and I would be lying if I said that being on TV doesn't make you self-conscious about your looks sometimes. It takes a while to get used to seeing yourself on screen, and it takes willpower and practice not to be too self-critical. It's human nature to want to look your best, though, so in the early days I'd be really careful to wear clothing styles I thought suited me, and tried to work out the most flattering ways to wear my hair.

Of course by far the most emails are directed against the female presenters. It's a rare day when one of my male colleagues gets criticised for how he looks, what he wears or his hairstyle.

Fortunately, I have always been reasonably confident about my appearance. I put that down to my upbringing — my parents were always far more focused on what we were doing with our lives than what we looked like. I'm no model — I've always been a sporty build, a size 12 on a good day, with all the curves you might expect of a mother of three in her late thirties. I guess you would call me 'body confident' because I'm lucky enough never to have been tortured by the way I look or a drive to be super-thin. If I can wear my jeans comfortably, then I'm pretty happy.

I'm also lucky I have Matt, who genuinely couldn't care less what size I am.

Of course there are days when I would love to look like Jessica Alba in my togs, but then I remember how much I love wine, and I'm never going to be someone who turns down a piece of birthday cake for fear of the calories.

I haven't talked publicly about this before, but when I was eighteen I had some fairly major plastic surgery. From the minute I started puberty, when I was about twelve, my boobs just grew and grew, by the time I was sixteen they were *huge*. It's no surprise, really — Mum is the same and so was my Nana June. But by the time I was in sixth form (year 12) I was wearing a size 12F bra. What bothered me most was the impact on my sport. The higher up the ladder I went, the worse it got. My back ached, my posture was bad and my boobs were really beginning to slow me down on the netball court and cricket field. I would wear two sports bras at once just to give them more support. And forget about being able to buy pretty lingerie; it was all about function for me.

The turning point came when my netball coach from the Canterbury Under-19 team called Mum and gently asked if we had ever considered a breast reduction. I didn't know such a thing existed, but the coach had had the operation years earlier and she said it had transformed her life.

She followed up the phone call with before-and-after photos, because she believed strongly that I should get this done. Mum had spent her whole life dealing with the aches and pains that come with a big bust, so she was very quickly keen on the idea. She asked whether it was something I would consider.

I was a bit scared, of course, because who wants to go under the surgeon's knife just for smaller boobs, but in the end I decided to go for it. My chest had attracted a lot of unwanted attention in my teens, and if it helped me in my sport it would be worth it. My parents forked out $12,000 for the operation, which was so generous. I remember Mum saying to me, 'I don't want you dealing with what I have all my life.' She could have used the money to have the surgery herself, but I guess that's what mothers do — put their kids' needs first. Certainly my mum does.

I had the surgery in the October university holidays, and it wasn't as big a deal as I had feared. I wouldn't recommend googling the operation, though. It's pretty rough and gory and seeing those images wasn't particularly helpful at the time. I remember the hardest part to get my head around was how they would cut around my nipples and take them off during the operation.

I spent one night in hospital and Mum looked after me at home while I recovered. The day the bandages came off was pretty amazing. I was swollen and had a drain hanging out the side of each boob, but even so, my body suddenly looked in proportion. They took 800 grams out of one side and 1.2 kilograms out of the other. I couldn't believe it! I hadn't realised how top-heavy I had been, but now I looked — well, pretty standard! I had gone from an F cup to a C.

Pretty much overnight the back pain and aching shoulders were gone, and the deep grooves in my shoulders from my bra straps began to fade. I could now wear one bra rather than two. I could sprint around the netball court and run between the crease without nearly whacking myself in the face, and new clothes fitted me properly. I could also pick cute little colourful bras from the teen section, and they didn't even need underwire — hallelujah!

I sometimes wonder how I would have negotiated my larger boobs with my TV job. It would have been a nightmare trying to get clothes that fitted properly, and viewers would have told me all about it.

It's sad how obsessed society is with appearance. Diet

and exercise were big topics in our house growing up. Mum always struggled with her weight and was always trying some new diet — whatever was in fashion at the time. But she was careful about how she framed any diet chat around us kids, and made sure the focus was on health and fitness rather than how we looked. We were encouraged to play sport in order to stay fit and healthy, not to be thin. We would go for runs with Dad because we knew it gave us a better chance of performing well at our chosen sport.

And let's face it, growing up in Taranaki, image and fashion were never much of a consideration. We just kicked around in clothes that Mum whipped up for us on her Bernina. New Plymouth in the early 1990s was no fashion Mecca, but I thought I was pretty cool in my homemade fluoro tracksuit. That was until about standard four, when all that was shattered. A boy in my class ran up to me in the school playground one day and said, 'Why are all your clothes so old? Why don't you wear any labels?'

I didn't know what 'labels' were, but I went home and interrogated Mum about why we were the only kids in homemade outfits. I suddenly saw her amazing seamstress skills in a horrible new light, and for the first time I realised there were ways of dressing that made you cool, and ways that made you decidedly uncool. Those neon trackies, it turned out, were in the latter camp.

To my pragmatic mum's eternal credit, she took me into

town and bought me a cream-coloured top emblazoned with JUST JEANS, a pair of forest-green shorts and a Kadu T-shirt (I will *never* forget it) from the local surf shop. I returned to school the next day feeling very chic in my new kit and was rewarded with an approving nod from the boy who had teased me.

I was relieved at the time, but I look back now and think 'Damn him' because everything changed from that moment. A childhood innocence was gone, and in its place was the start of that teenage angst about what you're wearing and how you look.

Marriage & Motherhood

Matt and I had talked a lot about marriage. We're traditionalists, so it was something we both wanted and knew would happen one day. The fact we were 'the one' for each other was never in question and I felt incredibly lucky to have found him. I wasn't in a hurry, though; I was far too focused on my new career to be thinking about weddings or babies or any of that stuff.

When we arrived back at the family farm for Christmas at the end of 2007 I was shattered. It had been a huge year: I had travelled extensively over New Zealand covering netball and other sporting events. I was totally spent and this holiday couldn't have come soon enough. Which might explain why I was not particularly receptive to being woken early the morning after we arrived. I needed to stay asleep, I told Matt.

'Just come outside with me,' he whispered. 'I've got something to show you.'

I don't remember my reply but it wasn't very polite. He was insistent, though, and eventually I dragged myself out of bed, half-asleep, and followed him out to the back lawn. There I saw he had laid out a picnic blanket and prepared us an outdoor breakfast. I looked at him in confusion.

'What's going on?' I asked. I couldn't be bothered with this. It was cold, the grass was all dewy and I just wanted to go back to bed. I was grumpy and it was written all over my face.

Matt wasn't having it. He sat me down and started telling me how much he loved me. It finally dawned on me what was going on. I looked a fright — my hair was all over the place and I was wearing mismatched PJs.

Undeterred, Matt unfolded a piece of pink A4 paper and

took a deep breath. He had written me a poem, which ended with the words 'Will you marry me?'

I wasn't grumpy anymore — I was laughing, and couldn't believe he had managed to pull this off without me knowing.

'Are you going to say yes?' he asked, holding out a gorgeous diamond solitaire engagement ring.

'Yes!' I said, wrapping my arms around him.

Matt's proposal took me completely by surprise. I was happy, because I had no doubt we were going to spend our lives together, but I also remember thinking 'I'm only 24!' It felt young to be taking such a big step.

Matt had secretly talked to Dad the day before, but Mum was as surprised as I was. Matt and I celebrated at a fancy restaurant that night and I remember thinking how special the timing was, because it ensured that Christmas was joyful. It's usually the time of year when Stephen's loss is most keenly felt, but Matt's proposal provided the happiest distraction, and wedding-planning conversations started almost immediately.

We decided to marry in New Plymouth and set the date for two year's time. I think everyone would agree I was not a bridezilla. I was too busy at work to give the wedding organisation the attention it needed, to be honest, so I just let Mum take the lead, and neither Matt nor I was too worried about the details. Even if I had wanted to micro-manage, I simply didn't have time. Most of 2009 was spent working long hours and travelling to major sporting events, including a three-week trip to Manchester in England for the Netball World Series.

Three weeks before the wedding I was busy scripting a story at work when I got a panicked call from Mum.

'Dad's had a heart attack; he's being airlifted to Waikato Hospital.'

He had started having chest pains while mowing the lawns earlier that day. Mum took him straight to the doctor's, where things suddenly got worse and he was rushed to hospital. Once there, it was clear he was in full cardiac arrest, so he was taken by helicopter to Waikato Hospital for surgery.

I couldn't believe it. Dad was only 53 and was the fittest of all of us. I jumped up from my desk and leapt in a taxi straight to the airport. Mum and Kirsty were waiting for me in New Plymouth and we drove to Hamilton, just over three hours away. It was a sombre journey because we were all unsure what state Dad would be in when we arrived. There was almost a sense of resignation that tragedy had struck again, and I couldn't bear to think about what losing Dad would do to Mum. It was eight years since Stephen died and the emotions felt horribly familiar.

Dad has always been active. If he's not working on the

farm he's playing golf, going for a run, doing the garden or fixing something around the house. He's never been good at sitting down. But unbeknown to any of us he had serious blockages in his arteries, and doctors told us he had been a ticking bomb. It was only a matter of time before he had a heart attack.

At Waikato Hospital we were directed to the cardiac ward and couldn't believe it when we saw Dad sitting upright in bed smiling, well and truly alive. He was stable and awaiting surgery in the next few days. He was so lucky; none of us could believe it. He spent a week in hospital recovering. Matt and I thought we should postpone the wedding, but Dad wouldn't hear of it.

'Don't even think about it,' he insisted. So that was that: the wedding would go ahead. We were worried it would be too much for him, but when he got out of hospital he was back to his old antics of all work, no rest. He even insisted on building a huge wooden platform out of scaffolding planks for our marquee to sit on. In typical Taranaki style it had been pouring with rain all week, and he was worried the ground would be too mushy for the guests. Dad's stubborn, and there's no stopping him once he's made up his mind. Mum, Kirsty and I constantly nagged him to slow down but 'I'll be right' is Geoff Street's catchcry.

Despite torrential rain the day before, Matt and I were married on a hot, sunny December day in 2009. It was Mum and Dad's 28th wedding anniversary, and when we woke up that morning to a bright blue cloudless sky we knew it was going to be a special day.

Dad walked me down the aisle as Elvis Presley's 'Can't Help Falling in Love' filled the Holy Trinity Church. Sun was filtering through the stained-glass windows, I was clutching Dad's arm, and I looked out to see all my friends and the people I loved sitting in the pews.

Dad's heart attack had served as yet another reminder of how quickly things can change and how lucky we were to have the people who were in our lives. I looked ahead at Matt, waiting at the front of the church with a huge grin spreading across his face, and felt awash with happiness. Not to mention a little uncharacteristically nervous for a person who worked every day in the public eye.

In front of 120 friends and family the two of us promised to stick together forever. It was in that moment, holding tightly onto Matt's hands, that I was struck with the momentousness of making these promises to the man I loved. The power of what we were doing hit me and nothing had ever felt more right. I was only 26 but I had complete and utter faith in this man before me, whose promises I knew he would keep. He was as solid as they come. Whatever was waiting for us in the future, we were approaching it together and I knew he would always have my back.

On that love-filled day we were also thinking of the people we had lost. It was hard not to. Matt's dad, our grandparents, Stephen, Lance and Tracy . . . They all should have been there. That's the thing about grief — it has a habit of gatecrashing happy occasions.

We had talked a lot about how we would acknowledge the sadness we all knew would be lingering in the background. We decided to embrace it. During the ceremony my bridesmaid, Renee Wright, chimed a crystal bell in honour of the loved ones we had lost, and Mum and Matt's mother, Mary, each lit a candle of remembrance. Stephen's best friend, Chad Mills, read a special verse. I found it incredibly emotional seeing this strapping 21-year-old standing at the front of the church, so grown-up and handsome in his suit. It just made me long for my little brother. He should have been at my wedding, and I felt sad that Matt and Stephen never had a chance to know each other. They would have got on so well, I just know it.

The reception was held at a beautiful venue called Barton Estate, which overlooked New Plymouth and the Tasman Sea. We made sure it was a party to remember. The marquee was decorated with huge urns of flowers, fairy-lights and a million tea-light candles that flickered in the fading light. One of the best parts of the day was a complete surprise for Matt and me. Mum and Dad had organised three old-school Yak warplanes to do a flyover while the guests were having drinks and canapés. At first the sound freaked everyone out — were we being attacked?! — but as they got closer everyone roared with approval. It was an awesome way to kick off the reception.

I loved every minute of the day.

Matt and I settled into married life. We bought our first home and I continued to work long hours at TVNZ. I had started to be called upon for the odd presenting shift, too. Initially I filled in for Tony Veitch, Andrew Saville and Jenny-May Clarkson on the sports desk. Then I got a chance to fill in for the first time on *Breakfast*, and that led to a regular gig covering for Petra Bagust every second Friday. The following year — when I was 40 weeks' pregnant! — I was offered the permanent hosting role.

It was a huge deal for me getting that job, and once I came back after maternity leave I learnt so much about presenting from those three hours' live television each morning. The (very) early starts were gruelling, but as long as I went to bed early I was fine. Discipline in that regard was key, and fortunately I had Matt's amazing support at home. He loves a strict routine, so he sent me to bed at 8.30 each night and constantly reminded me of the importance of daytime naps.

Still to this day I think *Breakfast* is one of the best — and most challenging — jobs in television, because it requires you to be nimble enough to handle a huge variety of topics, crossing seamlessly from one to the next for three hours solid. You have to be frivolous one minute and deadly serious the next. You need to be well-researched and competent enough to interview the prime minister about foreign policy and economics, yet have the relatability and warmth for the human-interest stories.

You have to have extraordinary stamina for three hours of live television, and the ability to work out how to make it all look effortless. It wasn't easy, but I absolutely adored that job.

Matt played for North Harbour until a back injury forced him into early retirement. He was gutted, because until then he had been working so hard to secure a Super Rugby contract and he was definitely good enough – he'd played the odd game for the Crusaders and Chiefs to cover injuries — but his dodgy back let him down. Fortunately he knew professional athletes always needed a Plan B, so he had been working as a town planner around his rugby.

Having a baby had always been in our plans and we didn't want to leave it too long. In my head I had set a deadline of age 30 for my first baby, so at 28, two years into married life, I was over the moon to find out I was pregnant.

This baby was not just for me and Matt; it was for my whole

family. I knew my parents would make amazing grandparents, and so would Matt's mum, Mary. I hoped a baby would bring joy to everyone.

I was astounded at how it felt to be carrying a new life for the first time. I hadn't even met this baby yet but I loved her so fiercely, and that gave me a deeper understanding of the loss my mother had endured. It was another reminder that love and grief so often go hand in hand.

Quite early in my pregnancy I wrote Mum a letter, telling her I had a new appreciation of not only how much she had lost, but also the extraordinary resilience she had shown. I knew her pain had lessened over time, but it still deserved to be acknowledged, especially now I knew what carrying a child felt like. Being pregnant gave me a whole new appreciation of just how much Mum and Dad had lost.

From a career perspective, I would have to say it was not ideal to be pregnant.

When I looked around the newsroom I didn't see many women successfully balancing career and family, and flexible working hours weren't really a thing back then. I hadn't worked this hard to walk away from my career now, but there were moments when I struggled to see how I could continue to be the kind of journalist I wanted to be when I had a baby at home. If you're out covering an unfolding story it's a bit tricky to take off halfway through to pick up a child on time. And then there was all the travel . . .

But I never considered postponing motherhood. It was just a matter of working out how I would juggle it with my career. First, though, I would have twelve weeks' maternity leave.

Juliette Ellen France was born on 4 October 2012. I know all parents say this, but I genuinely hadn't known I would love her so much. Matt and I became *those* parents — utterly smitten, totally obsessed and in our own little bubble.

She was perfect. She had strawberry blonde hair, pale skin, dark, soulful eyes and a knowing look that implied she was aware of what her presence meant to us all. I remember soon after she was born, as we took in every single tiny feature, she seemed to be doing the same to us. One of the doctors at the hospital told me she seemed like an old soul. When I told Mum, she said people used to say that about me when I was little.

We called her Baby Rhino — after me, apparently, because Matt always reckons I stomp around the house in the mornings. From the moment our Baby Rhino arrived she filled our lives with joy. The labour, predictably, had been fairly horrific — fifteen hours of agonising contractions until an epidural brought sweet relief. But other than the usual sleepless nights and first-time parent angst, she was a dreamy little thing. I would rush to her in the mornings and her face would light up with the biggest smile when she saw me.

I always knew Matt would make a wonderful dad, but he turned out to be even more than I expected. The only way to describe it is to call him a natural father. He seemed to know Juliette and her needs by intuition. Even when she was a newborn I never felt that I knew her better or had a deeper connection because I was the mother. Matt could always tell what her cries meant — whether she was hungry, tired or needed a nappy change. His swaddling skills were impressive too and she settled as easily for him as she did for me.

From the very start we were equal in our parenting, breastfeeding aside of course. It wasn't like we discussed and divided the duties; it just seemed to evolve that way. And I'm so thankful it did because it set us up so well for my return to work.

I had been flabbergasted when I was offered the hosting role on *Breakfast* — it was literally on Juliette's due date and I was a puffy whale at the time! I had loved filling in and doing the weekend show, but I thought I was still firmly regarded as a sports reporter and hadn't realised I was in line for a permanent presenting job.

There was no way I wanted to turn down this job, but I was terribly nervous about how I would cope going back to work so soon. I'd never been a mum before and I really had no idea what it would be like.

Matt and I came up with a plan. We would hire a nanny part time to cover until I got home. It was a wrench going to work and leaving my baby when she was so young, but the *Breakfast* hours actually worked brilliantly because I was home by 11 a.m. and had the rest of the day to spend with my girl. Had the *Breakfast* gig not been offered to me, I was planning to take twelve months of maternity leave, but that all changed after one meeting.

While I had this simplistic vision of Juliette's arrival helping to heal my family's wounds, things were of course more complicated than that. Mum never told me at the time, but while becoming a nana brought her great happiness, it also dredged up sadness that she thought she had dealt with. It started when I got pregnant, apparently, resurrecting memories for her of when she had Tracy. Tracy's was the loss she never grieved properly, she realised, and suddenly, 25 years on, the pain was raw again.

Difficult emotions around Stephen also resurfaced. Even though he had been gone for ten years, his bedroom remained completely untouched, and Mum and Dad finally decided they needed to clear it out to make space for grandchildren. His bed still had his old Tasmanian devil duvet cover, his wardrobe was full of his clothes and sports gear, and his Nokia phone still sat in the top drawer of his bedside table — alongside rugby cards, school books and things he'd collected over the years.

It was like a little museum to Stephen, but the room certainly hadn't been off-limits during that decade. It was a place to go to remember him and the things he loved. Mum always knew the time would come when she would need to deal with that room, and Juliette's imminent arrival was the catalyst.

But she wasn't ready and it really messed with her head. Mum says she now wishes she had held off. She didn't tell me any of this at the time, because she didn't want to taint my excitement about becoming a mum. Amid all the happy excitement, here was our old friend grief making another unwelcome and unbidden return. We all like to feel in control of our emotions, but I have learnt that you don't get to choose when you feel things.

It was around this time, when Mum was really struggling, that she read a story in the newspaper about a man who had lost his daughter. The part that struck Mum was when he said it had taken him thirteen years to stop feeling sad. Thirteen years. It sounds daunting, but for Mum it was vindication. Perhaps it's normal to feel this way for so long, she thought. And strangely, when the thirteen-year mark came around after Stephen's death, she felt the sadness lift a little.

She realised she was beginning to have more happy times

than sad — the balance was tipping. She now tells anyone else struggling with grief to be kind to themselves and accept that it's a long process. There is no shame in grieving; you can take as long as you need.

I think
I'm dying

'This baby is almost too good to be true,' I said to Matt one evening soon after bringing home our second beautiful baby girl. Mackenzie Kay France was born on 31 March 2015, and from the moment she arrived she just seemed at ease with the world. Calm and content, she fed and slept well; I remember thinking how much more relaxed it was for everyone the second time around.

We called Mackenzie our 'little hootie owl' because she had these big blue eyes and some of the chubbiest cheeks you'll ever see on a baby — she looked just like a Cabbage Patch Kid.

With your second baby there's not so much of that first-time angst, and I was so looking forward to having a more relaxed experience. Breastfeeding was easier this time — everything was. I had taken longer off work than I had with Juliette so we could lap up those precious first weeks. As I'm sure other working parents will agree, the prospect of having a break from the treadmill to focus entirely on family was so special. I craved it. I had been counting down and was beyond excited to be a stay-at-home mum for a while.

In between Juliette and Mackenzie, after less than a year on *Breakfast*, I had been offered the co-hosting role on *Seven Sharp* alongside Jesse Mulligan and Mike Hosking. This was the last thing I had been expecting. There had been no prior discussion — absolutely no hint that I might be in line for this promotion.

I was loving *Breakfast* and changing jobs wasn't on my radar at all. Juliette was still a baby and the *Breakfast* hours worked well with my role as a mum. I also had great friendships with my co-hosts Rawdon Christie, Sam Wallace and Nadine Higgins, and loved my executive producer, Antony Stevens. I know I should've been excited and flattered, but this wasn't how I'd planned things!

The new *Seven Sharp* show hadn't found its feet after its first year, and management decided they needed to change things. Never in a million years had I thought I would be involved in those changes, so I listened in disbelief as I was told they wanted a new panel of hosts, including Jesse from the original team, Mike (whom I'd never met), and me.

I could have said no, but I knew I'd have to be crazy to turn down a prime-time role like this. So, even though I was nervous and felt out of my depth, I sucked it up and accepted the job. At the same time I really felt for the team who were on their way out. They had only been doing the show for a year. It was tough.

Jesse was already a staff favourite at *Seven Sharp*. He is such a lovely guy and we instantly got on well. I was sad to see him leave the show only a few months later.

Mike was a more intimidating broadcaster. Aside from a couple of casual 'hellos' in passing in the TVNZ newsroom, I first met him at a photo shoot for our publicity material. It was bizarre — we'd only just met and yet here we were cuddling up for a photographer like the best of mates. He was probably thinking 'Whoa, this girl's full on', because I went straight in for a hug. In my mind, we had to get this chemistry started, and I must admit I felt totally at ease around him from the beginning.

I knew Mike was the right person for the job. He had been the regular fill-in for Mark Sainsbury on *Close Up* and he always rated well. I was excited about working alongside him. He's a love-him-or-hate-him kind of broadcaster, but a show like that needed someone with his reputation and gravitas to turn the ratings around.

Mike told me early on that it didn't matter whether people liked or didn't like you; what mattered was that they had an opinion. You wanted the viewer to *feel* something when they listened to you. The last thing you wanted was to be 'vanilla' — someone viewers thought was 'okay'. Mike was polarising, for sure, but people definitely watched him.

Over the coming months Mike's style gave me confidence to express my own opinions on things and I knew I needed to give my own views alongside his strong stances. He helped me show a bit of conviction, which was needed in that 7 p.m. slot. The producers introduced a segment at the end of the show where Mike and I gave our opinions on a topic of the day. That really helped me hone my thinking: I had to be clear in my opinions, and brave enough to take a position. Having trained and worked as a journalist it felt unnatural at first, because we're meant to be impartial, but media has changed a lot over the years. In many instances now we're increasingly encouraged to give opinions, which we would never do in straight news reporting.

After *Breakfast*, it took me a while to get my head around the 30-minute format, and for the entire first year it felt quite unnatural. I had gone from hosting a three-hour live show where we talked constantly to a much shorter show in which it felt like you had next to no time to make an impact. It was hard learning to work within such tight time constraints. If you stuffed it up you didn't get a chance to redeem yourself until the next show.

I remember coming home after many *Seven Sharp* shows and telling Matt I didn't feel as if I had said much. I often wondered whether I was contributing enough.

However, the ratings soon told us we were doing well, which was hugely encouraging. The bosses were happy and Mike and I were thrilled. I've always tried not to worry too much about ratings, but when they're going well it's very reassuring and motivating.

I had some amazing experiences on *Seven Sharp* and met some huge stars — Billy Crystal, Justin Timberlake (I tripped up the stairs as I walked towards him!), Ricky Martin, Ed Sheeran, Katy Perry, P!nk . . . it all felt pretty amazing for a girl from the provinces, and I have never lost that sense of 'Oh my god, how is this my job?'

By the time Mackenzie was born I had a year of *Seven Sharp* under my belt, was well embedded and felt confident in my role, so the 'return to work' deadline wasn't hanging over my head the same way it was after Juliette's birth.

Even the birth itself was less intense with Mackenzie. I joke that Juliette's head was bigger — actually it's no joke, it was apparently in the ninetieth percentile — so she paved the way and Mackenzie just slipped on through. (But only after hours of horrendous contractions — let's not gloss over that. It's awful.) I had also cracked my tailbone during the first birth, which meant sitting down was really painful for about six weeks, but I had none of that with baby number two, so physically I felt far more resilient afterwards.

I'm not a particularly superstitious person, but it's almost as if Mickey was born with the perfect temperament for the storm that was to come. She was happy in anyone's arms, didn't mind taking the bottle, and would fall asleep pretty much anywhere and on anyone. She was a little angel. Mum and Dad brought Juliette to meet her little sister at the hospital, and she just adored her from the beginning. We were worried there might be jealousy but it was the opposite. In Juliette's mind she was just like us, another parent, and Mackenzie was her little cub to protect. It made our hearts melt.

Then, after three wonderful weeks with our beautiful little girl, I started feeling sick.

It came on pretty slowly — a niggling pain at the top of my abdomen. At the start I ignored it, thinking it was residual indigestion from when I was pregnant. It was weird, though, because I had barely had indigestion during this pregnancy.

I'm an expert at downplaying symptoms. It was simply a side effect of the pregnancy; my body was exhausted from the whole process. And let's be honest, no mother has time to focus on her own problems while caring for a baby and a toddler. It would have had to be something *major* for me to go to the doctor. But I also have this ridiculous habit of ignoring uncomfortable things in the hope they'll somehow magically disappear. This is definitely not an approach I am proud of — nor would I recommend it to anyone else — but it's just the way I'm wired. I remain firmly in denial until it becomes glaringly obvious to everyone around me that I'm falling apart.

After a week I was chewing Quick-Eze like lollies and slugging back Gaviscon and neither was making any difference. I finally had to admit this was getting the better of me, so I booked in to see my GP, thinking they would prescribe something similar but stronger and I'd be good to go.

I was given a prescription for Losec, a heavier-duty indigestion medication, and I went home relieved. But the Losec made no difference at all to my symptoms. Now I was starting to worry, as was Matt; in fact he was more concerned than I was (the story of our lives!).

The burning pain at the top of my stomach was getting worse by the day. I put on a brave face, but that became harder and harder to maintain. The problem was that the pain was sporadic, so there were periods of time — a few hours, even — when I would feel completely fine. That convinced me it couldn't be anything too bad, because if it was the pain would be constant, surely?

I went back to a GP again, only to be told to give it a few more days and come back if it didn't get better. I had no idea what was happening to me, and my doctor seemed to know no more than I did.

The days were bearable but the nights were horrendous. I would go to bed hoping maybe tonight won't be so bad, but within a couple of hours I'd wake up in agony. It felt like the inside of my stomach was on fire and it escalated to the point where sleep was impossible. I was climbing the walls with the pain and the only thing that helped was being in hot water.

So when the pain reached its climax in the wee small hours, I'd crawl into the bathroom, turn on the shower, curl up under the water in the foetal position and stare at the white tiled walls. I'd stay there for hours, letting the warm water wash over me — not great for the power bill, but I didn't have the capacity to care about that at the time.

Matt would put his head around the corner into the ensuite to check on me.

'Can you help me?' I'd whisper, tears streaming down my

face. 'This is so so, bad, it's like nothing I've ever experienced.' But there was nothing he could do. I would send him back to bed because we both knew Mackenzie would be waking soon for her next feed and he needed some sleep first. I felt so useless, not being available for my newborn, so I needed Matt to take that burden from me. That's all I cared about in those helpless times when I couldn't get off the shower floor.

This went on for nearly two weeks. The daytimes became a blur — I was exhausted and sore, and freaking out about what was wrong with me. Every morning Matt and I would have the same conversation: 'Last night was horrific, but I actually feel a bit better this morning so let's see how tonight goes.' Looking back, it's obvious I should have consulted a specialist sooner, but we weren't thinking clearly. We were just getting from day to day — and neither of us wanted to face up to how serious this might be. Matt had just started a new job as an events manager with Netball New Zealand which was pretty full-on. The timing couldn't have been worse. He felt terrible about leaving me during the day, and I felt awful that I was adding to the pressure on him.

In the midst of this nightmare was two-year-old Juliette, who still needed her mum, and little Mackenzie, our brand-new baby. I was breastfeeding her, but there was no way I could keep going. I couldn't even lift her out of the cot. This was crushing for me because it felt so important. I would say melodramatic things to Matt, like, 'My daughter isn't even going to know who I am!' He would tell me not to be silly, but I couldn't shake the anxiety.

The days started to merge together and I was getting sicker by the minute. Things were spiralling and we didn't know what to do next.

Matt was scared. He didn't let on, but he must have secretly spoken to my parents because they cut short a holiday in Australia to come and help us. 'I'll be fine,' I tried to tell Mum over the phone, but she knows me too well. They changed their bookings and flew home.

Here was something else for me to feel guilty about — ruining their holiday and causing them yet more worry and heartache. Hadn't they been through enough?

They came straight to our house from the airport, and they got a real fright when they saw me. 'We're taking you to hospital,' Mum said. They dropped their bags and made it clear there was no alternative. Deep down I knew I had reached the point where I badly needed help too.

A huge sense of relief washed over me as Mum and Dad drove me to hospital. Matt stayed home with the kids so I didn't need to worry about them for now. For the first time I felt like we had a plan and we would get this problem sorted, whatever it was. Mum is great in a crisis and I felt reassured that she had taken charge of the situation. I was in no position to advocate for myself.

The week that followed turned out to be one of the lowest of my life. In the Emergency Department they wanted to assess my pain level, but I found it really hard to explain because I was running back and forth to the bathroom to vomit. I told them my pain was 8/10 and Mum said, 'It must be bad if Toni's saying eight.' Did I mention my ridiculous tendency to downplay things? I had also given birth only weeks earlier and that pain was fresh.

I was monitored in ED until the next morning when I was admitted to a ward. Initially they treated me for indigestion, just as the GP had, which was annoying because it was pretty clear by now that it wasn't that. The doctors kept prescribing a drink called Pink Lady, which is a disgusting concoction of indigestion and painkiller medication. It didn't do anything.

Specialists would come and ask me more questions, take more bloods, but days went by and still no one had any answers. The pain was becoming indescribable — the intense burning in my abdomen made me feel like passing out. They just kept plying me with paracetamol and Losec, and by this stage it was making both Mum and me pretty angry. 'For god's sake, it's not indigestion!' I felt like screaming. But I didn't; I knew they were trying their best.

An ultrasound ruled out gallstones. The blood tests continued. It felt as if litres and litres of blood were taken out of me as they went through the laborious process of ruling things out, one by one. Finally the pain became so intense I was put on a morphine drip. They hadn't wanted to do this because I was breastfeeding, but that seemed insane to me — I couldn't sit upright or even hold my baby, let alone latch her onto the boob! I am quite happy to admit that breastfeeding was pretty low on my priority list at this point. My baby was doing just fine on formula, and we had absolutely no choice in the matter anyway. I was in no fit state to feed a baby.

The morphine helped to mask the pain, but as soon as it wore off the horribly familiar agony would return.

The doctors were now worried about a new symptom — an angry rash all over my legs. It was red and blotchy and they wondered if I was having an allergic reaction to some of the pain meds. No one had a clue. I was a mystery.

I was so sick that when Mum brought Mackenzie in to see me I looked at her and turned away. I didn't have the energy to hold her and cuddle her — this perfect little baby I had given birth to only a few weeks earlier. I was the same with Juliette. Mum and Matt would bring her to see me, but I barely had the strength to engage with her. For a mother, that's the worst feeling in the world. Seeing them was a reminder of what I was missing.

That week in hospital made me so vulnerable. I tried to tell them that I could feel something very, very bad was happening inside me, but it felt as if no one was listening. I'm sure they were doing their best but I just wanted to scream. I lay in that hospital bed crying, which was very uncharacteristic for me.

Six weeks ago I had been in that very hospital giving birth to a beautiful baby girl. Now I was too sick to even hold her.

My worst night on the ward came on about day two or three — the pain in my stomach was so intense I was writhing in agony, unable to eat, sleep or lie still. Suddenly I felt something really scary happening in my bowel. I don't know how I knew it was my bowel but I did, and I know it's gross but I truly thought it was going to explode. I desperately pressed the buzzer for help, and a nurse ran in to find me keeled over. I begged her to give me an enema — it was the only thing I could think of that would bring me relief because the pain was too much to bear. I had to get it out of me.

There was no enema and I can't even remember how that night ended; all I know is I was drugged up to the eyeballs on pain relief. I felt broken after that. I felt as if I was dying and I was all alone. I was starting to lose the plot emotionally, with a loop going around inside my head saying 'You're going to die and your babies will be left without a mum.'

Not one of the endless stream of doctors who examined me had any answers. I felt as if I had absolutely no control over what was happening to me — and nor did anyone else.

After another few days in hospital with no real change and no answers I was discharged. There was no discussion of any possible treatment, let alone a diagnosis, and the pain relief was the only thing keeping me going.

I was happy to be getting out of hospital because every

day there brought no hope whatsoever and I was desperate to be back with my babies. But at the same time, Matt and I were terrified about what going home meant for us. I was scared of being without morphine.

Did I believe I was miraculously going to improve? No way. It felt like I was being packed off home to die. I know that sounds melodramatic, but that's how low I was feeling. I was teary all the time and tormented by the need to find out what the hell was wrong with me. If a week in hospital couldn't help, what on earth would?

For a couple of days after getting home I rallied. The painkillers were doing their job and I was so happy to be at home with Juju and Mickey. I clung to the hope that everything was going back to normal. I certainly wasn't up to venturing outside, but I was able to sit on the couch and feed my baby a bottle and watch Juliette toddle around and play with her toys.

I knew I wasn't out of the woods, though. I know my body and I could feel that the reprieve was down to the painkillers. If I didn't down the next lot in time, things would quickly become unbearable again. After a day or two I was as sick as I had been in hospital. I was devastated but not at all surprised. I felt totally hopeless again.

Matt was amazing throughout. In a crisis he goes into military mode — focused, calm and determined. I know when he's stressed, but he's not a panicker and that is a huge help in keeping everyone else calm. (It has been said that I'm the dramatic one in our relationship . . .)

Amazingly, the girls seemed largely unaffected by what was going on. In fact Juliette was on cloud nine because Nana and Grandad were staying with us full time. We had explained to her that Mummy was a bit sick, but that means nothing to a two-year-old. Toddlers are adorably self-centred.

I am forever grateful to Matt for keeping their lives as normal as possible throughout that tumultuous time. Despite all the stress, he kept playing with them and laughing and making sure they were not affected. He's an incredible dad.

Not that they let on, but I know my parents were frightened. Once again they were dealing with a sick child. I don't think it makes a difference whether that child is small or an adult, that fear is still there. I was only too aware of being another burden for them.

A glimmer of light finally appeared at the end of the tunnel when my obstetrician, Dr Ammar Al-Abid, the man who had taken such good care of me during both pregnancies and deliveries, phoned to see how I was doing after hearing of my plight in hospital.

'I'm not great at all,' I said, my voice decidedly wobbly. He had caught me at a low moment and I ended up telling him the whole story. He told me I *must* go and see his childhood friend from Iraq, a gastroenterologist named Dr Ali Jafar who now practised in Auckland. 'He will sort you out,' Ammar insisted.

He sounded so sure about this that for the first time in weeks I felt a tiny spark of hope — and man, did I cling to that. Two days later, when I met Ali, I had a strong sense that I was in safe hands — finally.

Dr Ali Jafar looked me in the eyes and said, 'Don't worry, we are going to get to the bottom of this. We will find out what's wrong.' He was softly spoken, thoughtful and kind, and almost instantly that feeling of being out of control ended. I completely and utterly trusted that this man was not going to rest until he found out what was wrong with me.

This felt like the turning point and I was so incredibly lucky to have found Ali. It was one of those sliding-door moments. If Ali hadn't gone to medical school in Iraq with Dr Ammar Al-Abid, and if they hadn't both decided to move to Auckland, New Zealand . . . If I had chosen a different obstetrician during my first pregnancy, I might never have ended up with Ali. I owe this man so much.

Mum came with me to that first appointment, and I remember saying to her before we walked in: 'If this guy doesn't know what's wrong with me, we're out of options. There's nowhere else we can go.' I wasn't in a great mental state, to be honest. I had used up all my positivity — the tank was empty. I was on the verge of tears as I walked into his office, and Mum wasn't much better.

The first thing Ali did was lie me on the bed and feel my tummy. Then he immediately said, 'You have a very sick gall bladder.' A week in hospital and no one had picked that up, but he knew immediately. 'You'll need to have a scan and likely an operation to have that taken out,' he said. Never have I been so relieved at the prospect of surgery. This was affirmative action at last, and if I could have booked the surgery for that afternoon I would have. In fact, I would have skipped into the operating theatre.

Ali had all my notes in front of him and had looked through my blood test results going back years and years. He saw that I had had sinus issues, allergic reactions, asthma and eczema. And he saw that the treatment for many of those ailments had been a short course of steroids — a short-term fix. This, it turned out, was a major clue.

It was a long appointment, during which Ali told me he suspected I was suffering from an autoimmune condition. He referred me to Rohan Ameratunga, an immunologist, and also to a gall bladder specialist, who booked me in for the scan within a couple of days. Even though I was still in pain I felt so much calmer for being in the care of this wonderful man. It's amazing the difference a little bit of hope can make.

I went to my first appointment with Rohan on my own. Matt was working, and I was sure I would be fine. Mum and Dad had dashed home to New Plymouth for a much-needed recharge after weeks of living with us. I was feeling so much stronger mentally now that I had a potential diagnosis, and from my own reading I was pretty sure Ali was right about the autoimmune condition. I wasn't sure what that meant, but I felt we were on the right track to getting me well.

So I was feeling hopeful when I walked into Rohan's office. Within minutes of my sitting down he told me he believed he had found a reason for my illness. He had pored over my notes, my blood test results and my medical history, and he was about to utter the words that would change my life.

'I think you have something called Churg-Strauss Syndrome.'

Huh, Churg-Strauss? I'd never heard of it. 'How do you even spell that?' I asked.

'Churg-Strauss is an inflammation of your blood vessels. It restricts the blood flow to your vital organs and can cause them permanent damage,' Rohan said.

What the hell?

'You are gravely unwell and we need to act quickly. We're going to get you started on chemotherapy as soon as we can.'

Chemotherapy — that's for people with cancer. That can't be me, I can't be that sick.

I'm normally quite calm and level-headed in a crisis but I started to panic, and tears were welling up. I felt dizzy and flustered and inside my head I cursed myself for not bringing Matt to the appointment with me. I needed him because I quickly started to despair. 'I'm going to die in my thirties and my girls won't have a mum,' I thought. 'My tiny baby won't even remember me.'

Rohan was still talking, eager to make sure I understood how serious this was and that we needed to make an action plan — today. He explained that my body was attacking itself, and my internal organs were in serious danger of failing. This guy didn't mince his words. There were eight markers for Churg-Strauss and I had seven of them.

'People do die from this,' he said.

In total disbelief, I asked Rohan what my life expectancy was. He said he wouldn't know my prognosis until he had found out the extent of damage to my organs. That would require testing every part of my body that may have been affected — heart, lungs, liver, kidney, bowel and nervous system. As Rohan gave me the cold, hard facts, his face was kind and sympathetic. I could tell he felt bad delivering my diagnosis.

I stumbled out of that appointment and sat in my car like a stunned mullet, wondering who to call first and what to tell them. It felt as if I had been given a life sentence. I could barely breathe. I had not been expecting anything like this, not in a million years. I knew very little about autoimmune conditions, and nothing about Churg-Strauss. All I could think was 'How can this be happening?' I wasn't scared for myself; I only cared about my girls being without their mum, and the rest of my family who would have to pick up the pieces.

Churg what?

I don't know why, but instead of calling Matt I rang Mum. There are certain times in life when you just need to hear your mum's voice and this was one of them. I was not in a good state. Through tears I tried to get out the words to tell her I was facing a life-threatening illness. 'I have to have chemo,' I sobbed. 'Rohan says some people die of this.'

Mum was amazing, as always. Calmly and firmly, she said, 'We will deal with this and it's going to be okay. Just get home and we'll be there soon. We'll deal with it.' I managed to drive home, where Matt was waiting for me. Mum had filled him in and, even though he must have been terrified, he was his usual calm, reassuring self. He held me while I cried and promised me we would get through it. Meanwhile, Mum and Dad were packing up the car in New Plymouth once again, putting their lives on hold to take over the reins of my family. Here I was putting more stress on them. I felt awful.

I know I shouldn't have done this, but I hit Dr Google in a big way. I needed to know everything about this thing that was making me so damned ill. I tried to stick to reliable sources, but even so it made for terrifying reading. 'Without treatment, the disease can be fatal,' I read. 'Churg-Strauss Syndrome is rare and has no cure.' 'Churg-Strauss varies greatly from person to person. Some people have only mild symptoms. Others have severe or life-threatening complications.'

Well, we all knew where I was on that spectrum. I learnt that the disease (also known as eosinophilic granulomatosis with polyangiitis, or EGPA), is part of the multiple sclerosis family. Everyone with the condition has asthma, chronic sinusitis and elevated levels of white blood cells called eosinophils, which in a healthy body help fight disease by curbing infection and boosting the body's immune response.

Mine were so high they had flooded my system, creating an overactive immune response which, without treatment, would cause my organs to fail, Basically it meant my body was attacking itself.

The more I read, the worse I felt, but I ploughed on, desperately searching for stories of hope among the many examples of Churg-Strauss sufferers who hadn't made it.

'Asthma usually begins five to nine years before the diagnosis of Churg-Strauss,' I read. This was a lightbulb moment. Suddenly it dawned on me that there had been clues all along that this thing started affecting me in my twenties. A whole bunch of little mysteries were beginning to be unravelled.

I had always been a healthy child and teenager. I hardly ever got sick and I never had sensitive skin or eczema or any of those things other kids seemed to get. I mean, I played representative sport for all those years and never got remotely wheezy or needed an inhaler. But when I was about 25 I developed asthma and eczema virtually overnight. They seemed to come from nowhere, arrived together and would flare up every few months. I would get covered in a dry, scratchy rash, always accompanied by coughing and wheezing. Each time it happened I would trot off to the doctor, get put on a course of oral steroids and given a concoction of ointments, and without fail my symptoms would settle. It did seem weird to have developed a whole new raft of problems out of nowhere, but I never for a moment imagined it was the start of something serious.

There were other clues in hindsight, too. Just a week or two after I gave birth to Juliette in 2012, I woke up with a really sore neck. I assumed I must have slept on it strangely, so I washed down a Voltaren anti-inflammatory and a Nurofen for the pain. It was a combo I had taken plenty of times over the years and it always did the trick. But this time, within about ten minutes of taking the pills I was vomiting. My throat felt as if it was closing over and I had an intense burning feeling in my stomach.

Matt was away in Japan for work, but luckily Mum was staying and she rushed me to the doctor. It was obvious to them I was having a severe reaction to something, so an ambulance was called and I was taken to North Shore Hospital. By the time I arrived, I was having a full-blown anaphylactic reaction to the combination of drugs. Doctors administered a hefty dose of oral steroids, and within minutes I started feeling a lot better. I left hospital several hours later thinking how bizarre it was to have that reaction to something I had taken so many times before.

Through my research into Churg-Strauss I discovered that my story wasn't unique — most people suffer from asthma, eczema and allergies for years before a diagnosis is made. Disturbingly, most people only find out they have Churg-Strauss at the point of heart failure, by which time it's usually not survivable. It was clear to me now that if it had reached my heart, I was in real trouble. I was petrified.

It's an awful feeling being faced with your own mortality, and as a mother my thoughts were focused purely on my girls. The idea of not being here for them was crushing.

The next few days after the diagnosis were a blur of pain and fear as I struggled to keep it together in front of all of my loved ones. I spent hours curled up on my bed, knocked for six by my symptoms and anxiety over what my looming tests might reveal. I felt utterly useless as I heard the rest of my family in the living room down the hall. Life was going on around me, but I wasn't able to be part of it.

Matt and Mum were doing all the parenting — I was too sick to help at all. This was my maternity leave, for goodness' sake; I should have been bonding with my baby, but instead I was either out having blood tests or seeing new specialists, or I was stuck on the couch, no use to anyone. The guilt I felt about not being there for my young family threatened to overwhelm me. Even though I was surrounded by love and support — not to mention so many amazing messages and presents and bunches of flowers from friends, family and work colleagues — I felt so alone. I longed to be a proper mum but I could barely even cuddle my kids. My milk had dried up during the hospital stay, so Mackenzie was now entirely bottle-fed. Even if I had tried to resume breastfeeding, the milk would have been laced with the cocktail of drugs I was on.

In my darkest moments my heart felt broken. But some days, when I was able to think with clarity, I felt nothing but gratitude for the love and support that filled our house. I knew my baby was happy as — I only had to take one look at that smiling, cooing little bundle of cuteness to know that. It was me who was struggling, not her.

Over the following fortnight I visited what felt like every medical specialist in Auckland to assess the extent of the damage to my internal organs. Matt and I barely slept. We were just going through the motions, one day at a time, trying not to think too far ahead. Thank goodness Mum was there to feed us and look after the kids, because we were in a state.

My first, and by far the most important, appointment was to check my heart function. My specialist and my own research had told me that if my heart was damaged, there would be implications for my life expectancy, so I guess it's understandable that I was worried. I was given an urgent appointment on a Saturday morning at a private cardiac clinic in Mt Eden. It was in a funny little old bungalow and the whole thing felt eerie. We were the only people in the waiting room, and there were only a couple of staff working. This of course added to my fear: clearly it must be serious if it couldn't wait until Monday.

I stripped off and put on a gown, and a doctor attached stickers and wires all over my body. I then walked on a treadmill for a cardiac stress test, where the speed is gradually increased to make my heart work progressively harder. An electrocardiogram (ECG) monitored my heart's electrical rhythms, and I was constantly asked if I was experiencing any chest discomfort or fatigue.

I'd just had a baby, so I wasn't in the fittest state I'd ever been, but I felt absolutely fine on that treadmill, which was reassuring. But I knew the real test was what showed up on the ECG, and I kept searching the doctor's face for clues. She was giving nothing away and it felt like the longest hour of my life. Finally, the treadmill slowed to a stop, I got dressed again and we sat down to discuss the results. 'That all looks normal,' she said, as Matt and I sat opposite him nervously. 'No sign of any problem.'

Oh my god! Did I hear that right? 'So there's no damage?' I asked, in disbelief.

'No sign of damage,' she confirmed.

Relief washed over me and I could have cried with joy.

Matt and I looked at each other silently. This was the best news: we had got over the first and biggest hurdle in terms of long-term damage

'This is huge, Tones,' Matt whispered as we walked out of the clinic. 'You're going to be fine; you're going to get through this.' Relief was written all over his face, too, and I knew in that moment how much he had been holding back from me. Matt would never have admitted it, but he had been just as worried as I was. We still had the rest of the tests to go, but the heart was the biggie. We could cope with damage to the other organs, but hearts are hard to fix.

It was no surprise to receive confirmation that my gall bladder was shot — Dr Ali had picked that. I just wanted the bloody thing out. The doctor explained that a sick gall bladder is often linked to severe anxiety, which came as no surprise to me. It was almost a relief to know there was a reason for my overwhelming feeling of doom, and an even bigger relief to hear that the anxiety should lift once the gall bladder came out.

Next was a gastroscopy (where a tiny camera is sent down your throat on a tube, for those of you unlucky enough not to have experienced this delightful procedure) to assess any damage to the stomach and small bowel. They saw clear evidence of streaking and scarring, indicating that the bowel had been attacked almost to the point of perforation. I'm convinced this is what was happening that awful night in hospital when I had the agonising sense that my bowel was going to explode. No wonder it had hurt so much! There was no treatment for this; we just had to wait for my body to heal itself.

With the gall bladder and bowel both affected, I wasn't feeling too hopeful for the next tests. But other than severe nasal polyps, which also required surgery, I finally started getting some lucky breaks. My lungs were unaffected, a bone-density scan found no sign of damage, my throat was fine, and my ears had been spared. My liver was given the all-clear and my kidneys, too. Hallelujah! Things were looking up.

Armed with all the test results I went back to see Rohan, who had copies in front of him. He was smiling as I walked into his office. Definitely a good sign.

'You're incredibly lucky,' he said, explaining that I had probably escaped worse damage because I was still relatively young. He also explained that having children had helped speed up my Churg-Strauss diagnosis because childbirth brings the symptoms to the surface. The immune system is suppressed during pregnancy so it doesn't attack the baby. But when it fires up again four to six weeks post-partum, Churg-Strauss patients can experience a big flare of symptoms, as I had after both my daughters' births. So I was actually fortunate, even though it certainly didn't feel like it at the time. If I hadn't had kids, and if the symptoms had presented later in life, things could have been a lot more serious. I had dodged a bullet, it seemed. I was overjoyed to hear that I would not need chemotherapy after all. 'That's not to say you might not need it further down the track,' Rohan quickly warned, 'but we'll start with steroids and see how we get on, how you respond.'

He explained that I was not out of the woods by any stretch, and that my prognosis depended on how well my

ABOVE LEFT Lance and me just before our first birthday.

ABOVE RIGHT Sharing an ice block two months before Lance died.

RIGHT Mum and six-year-old me heading out for dinner in Wellington.

OPPOSITE ABOVE First official Street family portrait, taken a couple of days after the news that Lance had relapsed.

OPPOSITE BELOW LEFT Stephen and me posing for the sibling kindy photo.

OPPOSITE BELOW RIGHT Christmas Day 1988 – Stephen and me snuggling in my bed with our new Minnie and Mickey Mouses we got for Christmas.

RIGHT Street family portrait.

BELOW Kirsty, Stephen and me all dressed up for more family photos.

LEFT Strutting my stuff down the runway at a Plunket fundraiser at three years old.

BELOW One of Mum's favourite photos of Stephen as a 10-year-old.

OPPOSITE ABOVE LEFT My favourite photo of Stephen and me messing around at home.

OPPOSITE ABOVE RIGHT Stephen and I loved pretending it was snowing when the cherry trees blossomed on the farm.

OPPOSITE BELOW Got 'em! The glory days playing cricket for Taranaki.

LEFT New Plymouth Girls' High School head girl, 2001.

BELOW Matt and me at my graduation day at Lincoln University.

OPPOSITE RIGHT Family holiday in Hawaii.

OPPOSITE BELOW Reporting on the World Netball Championships in Singapore, 2011.

ABOVE Reporting live for TVNZ's Olympics coverage from the Bird's Nest in Beijing, China, 2008.

BELOW The TVNZ America's Cup team reporting from San Francisco in 2013.

ABOVE Hosting breakfast TV live in the field with my executive producer Antony Stevens and co-host Rawdon Christie.

BELOW The *Seven Sharp* team in 2017.

OPPOSITE ABOVE Happy to be back at work and healthy with SOL3 MIO's Pene Pati and my Hits Breakfast co-hosts Sam Wallace and Laura McGoldrick.

OPPOSITE BELOW Pumped full of steroids and swollen celebrating the All Blacks' World Cup win while interviewing Beauden Barrett in 2015.

ABOVE LEFT Meeting Ed Sheeran on a trip to Melbourne with The Hits.

ABOVE RIGHT *Seven Sharp* shenanigans with Mike Hosking.

RIGHT Incredible trip to Los Angeles to interview P!nk for *Seven Sharp*.

LEFT With my maid of honour Sophie Braggins on Matt's and my wedding day in 2009.

BELOW Mr and Mrs France.

RIGHT Looking like a demon mid-way through my liver illness.

BELOW Trip to Noosa after IVF and steroid treatment with Juliette, my sister Kirsty and Mackenzie.

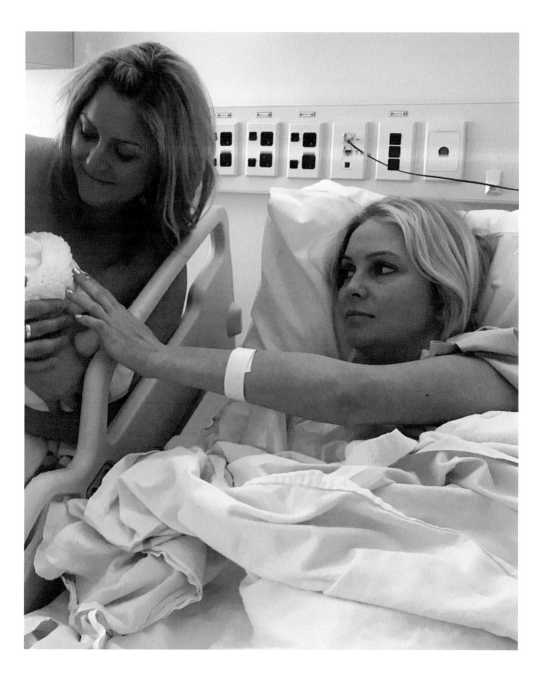

ABOVE A couple of hours after Sophie gave birth to Lachie.

ABOVE Snuggles with my baby Lachie.

RIGHT A special moment between Lachie and Sophie on holiday with the Braggins family.

LEFT In the Family Court on the day we adopted Lachie.

BELOW France family trip to Hobbiton.

body responded to treatment. I needed an intense course of methylprednisolone infusions — 1000 mg (1 gram) a day would be pumped into me via a drip for three consecutive days every month, for six months. Every other day I would take 40 mg of oral prednisone to keep me topped up.

To provide some context here, the usual treatment for a sinus infection might be a five-day course of 20 mg of prednisone.

The hope was that this mega-dose would reduce the inflammation levels throughout my body, but the only way to know would be through regular blood tests. By regular, he meant daily for the first few weeks, and weekly after that.

The side effects of long-term high-dose steroid treatment, he explained, could be significant. Patients may experience weight gain, hot flushes, mood disturbances, mania, sleeplessness, nausea, bone weakness, blood-pressure problems . . . the list went on. But in that moment I didn't really care. All I cared about was getting started so I could get well again and restart my life. I was so sick of being sick!

Rohan wasn't finished, though. I would also need a high dose of a drug called mycophenolate motefil (brand name CellCept), which, as anyone who has had a transplant will know, is a strong immunosuppressant used to prevent organ rejection. This came with another raft of side effects such as dizziness, nausea, diarrhoea, headaches, hair loss, insomnia and swelling.

I had no idea what was about to hit me, but it was enormously comforting to finally have a plan. I was going to get better.

I started the oral medication straight away, and within a day or two the burning in my stomach began to reduce. The clouds were parting and a little bit of sunshine was allowed in — it was the most blessed relief to have a break from the constant pain I had been living with for over a month. By the time of my first steroid infusion I was feeling positive and had almost forgotten Rohan's warning about side effects. Anyway, anything would be better than what I had been living with.

I was ushered into a little room off the side of Rohan's autoimmune clinic, where there were about five La-Z-Boy chairs lined up, each with a drip next to it and a chair for a support person. Matt and I took our places, and I watched as the nurse slid the needle easily into my arm. She attached the bag of medication to the catheter, hung it up on the stand, and I watched it slowly drip into my vein over the next two hours.

Within just a few minutes I started feeling weird — kind of like an electric current was running through me, and I had a distinct metallic taste on my tongue.

'Your face has gone bright red,' Matt said, looking slightly alarmed.

I wasn't surprised; my whole body was burning hot and

my skin was tingling. It stayed that way the whole time, and I figured that meant it was working at least. I left the appointment feeling stoked to have the first one under my belt. One down, many more to come.

For the first few weeks of treatment I was buoyed along by the euphoria of being free from my Churg-Strauss pain. I was aware of the steroid side effects creeping in, but it wasn't until about week four that they hit me hard. The nausea and upset tummy I could cope with; the emotional effects were harder to handle. One minute I was euphoric, the next I would be hit by a tidal wave of tiredness and irritability. I had a strange kind of energy running through me, which I guessed was the mania Rohan had mentioned. I felt I needed to be constantly doing something, and I became quite intense about housework. Matt would find me furiously cleaning the cupboards straight after work, or scrubbing the fridge out on a Sunday morning. I ran around all day doing things until I collapsed at night, and then I felt like death the next day, aware that I'd completely overdone it.

The longer my treatment went on, the worse it got, to the point where at times I felt I had completely lost control of my emotions. It was a scary feeling — in a way I felt as though I was losing my mind. It was like I was standing on the sideline watching someone else in my body.

I regularly felt inexplicably angry and unstable and on the verge of tears. I never did actually boil over because I internalised most of it. I didn't want anyone to fuss over me, even Matt, so I would go off and have a cry on my own in the shower. My other coping mechanism was to just sit still staring out the window until I felt better. I was determined not to be a burden — Matt and the rest of my family had been through enough. I kept comparing these side effects to how I felt when I was really ill before the diagnosis, and that made me feel better — at least I knew this was getting me well. The prednisone was a necessary evil, but being without the drugs was a kind of hell that I definitely didn't want to go back to.

The nights were tough because steroids interfere with your sleep. Sometimes I lay in bed for hours on end, eyes wide open and thinking manic thoughts. It was exhausting. I was still at the beginning of this treatment — would it get worse? How would I cope then?

I made a conscious decision to focus on one day at a time, which helped a lot. And Mum was always there, issuing her mantra for life. 'One foot in front of the other,' she would say when I was overwhelmed by it all. It didn't take much to tip me over. I'd get a beautiful message from a friend, or be watching Matt play with the girls, and the tears would come. It was a real lesson in how medication can change your mood, your state of mind and your personality as a whole.

At some point in all this I had to have the two surgeries — one to remove my gall bladder and the other to remove nasal polyps. I cheekily asked if they could be done at the same time so I only needed one round of general anaesthetic, but that wasn't a go. The surgeons probably thought I was a bit crazy for asking, but it would have saved me a lot of emotional energy.

The gall bladder came out first, and I was excited to see whether this would help reduce my anxiety. In fact I was hoping I would wake up from the anaesthetic feeling brand-new, but that didn't happen. The steroids had their own agenda in regard to my mental health.

The nasal operation was just a simple day surgery, which went well. The worst part was having to return to the clinic a few times during those six weeks in order for a large metal prong to be shoved up my nose to scrape out all the blood and scabs. It was hideous. You would think I would have a high pain threshold after what I had been through, but that prong felt like it was going halfway to my brain. I dreaded those appointments.

All the while, despite the side effects of the infusions, my daily blood tests showed an improvement in my eosinophil levels, meaning I was responding well to the treatment. I was thrilled, and secretly this gave me the first glimmer of hope that I might be able to return to work soon. I was keen to get back to *Seven Sharp* and back into a routine, and with Mickey four months old I had been planning to return from maternity leave about now.

Matt and Mum were sceptical, but every part of me longed for my normal life. I felt that if I could just get back to work, it would be a huge step towards getting everything back on track and formulating some sort of routine that didn't revolve around waiting to take my meds. I wanted my old life back.

I do have a habit of rushing into things, though, which drives Matt crazy, and it really got me into trouble with a promo shoot that had been scheduled months before any of this. It was a television advertisement with Māori TV, TVNZ and TV3, and it turned out it fell on the day after my gall bladder surgery. I decided I would be fine to do it.

Matt knew I had this thing booked and made it clear he thought it was insane to even consider working the day after an operation. He nagged me for weeks, but I kept refusing to pull the pin, mainly because I knew how many different organisations had committed to this date and I didn't want to let everyone down. I kept googling 'gall bladder surgery recovery time' and found examples of patients who had managed to go to work the following day. If they could manage it, I could too, I stupidly told myself, conveniently overlooking the new baby, the recent diagnosis of a life-threatening condition, the brain full of drugs, and the fact that I was probably weaker than I had ever been in my life.

With stitches fresh in my abdomen, I woke up the day after the operation feeling terrible. 'I'll be okay,' I told myself over and over, dragging myself to the bathroom to shower. But when my makeup artist for the shoot, Keryn, walked in the door she took one look at me and shook her head. 'Toni, you're completely green. You *cannot* go through with this.' Keryn is a TVNZ makeup and hair stylist and has worked with me for years, so she knew straight away that something was clearly not right with me. I think it was her look of disapproval that made me realise how stupid I was being.

The next minute I was in the toilet vomiting. I reluctantly agreed with Matt and Keryn that we should call the producers and tell them I couldn't do it. It was so embarrassing — the camera crew were setting up, the other talent were there, and because of my stupidity I had stuffed it up for everyone.

I learnt a big lesson that day. If I had listened to my body and to the people who loved me, I would have saved everyone a huge load of hassle. I felt like such an idiot.

The next few weeks were pretty tough as I recovered from the two operations and continued with the steroid treatments. By now, the steroid side effects were in full flight. I'd feel really good for a couple of days, I'd get some exercise in, have lots of energy for the kids, then I'd crash in a heap with extreme fatigue the next day. My back felt like the nerve endings were inflamed and it would hurt if anyone touched me. It was a real rollercoaster, physically and mentally.

I've always been a really good, solid sleeper, but I was surviving most of the time on about four or five hours' sleep a night. The rest of the night I lay awake, my brain buzzing. For someone who has always been relentlessly positive and pretty mentally stable it felt really scary. I've always been a naturally happy person but I was struggling to find the joy now, and there were a lot of days when I'd be super-flat, and no matter how hard I tried I couldn't pull myself out of it. Even though you know it's the medication, when you're in the middle of it all it's hard to rationalise your way out.

Being unwell with small children is tough because they don't understand. I had many moments of feeling miserable that I was missing a chunk of their little lives by being so ill. I felt cheated, especially when it came to Mickey, who was so little when I first got sick. She was totally unaffected, I knew that. She was a big chunky, happy baby, but it didn't stop me feeling like I was missing out somehow. It was hard to take it easy and rest when I desperately wanted to make up for lost time with her.

I am forever thankful to have had that month with her before I got sick because our bond was cemented then — she knew I was her mum. Juju was thriving, too. In fact I think she loved having the constant attention of her Nana and Grandad for two months! Like all grandparents, they spoiled her rotten and she adored them. It reminded me of my relationship with Nana June, who took care of me when Lance was ill. It's a beautiful thing to feel as safe with your grandmother as you do with your own mum, so how could I feel sad about that?

Juliette had the same relationship wih her Granny Mary too.

My appearance was changing, thanks to the steroids. My face had blown up like a balloon and I put on about 10 kilograms in the space of about eight weeks. A layer of blubber appeared around my middle. I know I had just had a baby, but this wasn't leftover pregnancy weight; it was like a swollen tyre and made me feel pretty gross, especially as I had piled it on so damned fast. When I looked in the mirror I did a double-take. I didn't look like me anymore — my features were being gobbled up by this big, round moon face. At times it looked like my eyes were disappearing into the puffiness. There's a photo I had taken with Beauden Barrett when the All Blacks returned with the 2015 Rugby World Cup. I looked so ill — it's a great reminder of how far I've come since.

In that photo I'm also wearing my hair far shorter than I normally do. That's because my hair had started falling out and I was forced to keep it short. I first noticed it in the shower a few weeks after my first infusion, when I reached up to rinse the shampoo out and came away with a clump of hair wound through my fingers. 'My hair is falling out!' I yelled to Matt in alarm. He took it all in his stride.

'Yeah, we knew that would happen,' he said. 'Rohan mentioned that.'

The hair loss got worse and worse — every morning I would check the pillow to see how much had come out overnight. After every shower the plughole would be full of it, and when I brushed I seemed to leave half my hair on the bristles.

In the space of a few weeks my thick, healthy mane became a tangled, brittle mess. It was so dry and damaged that the strands would snap like twigs, but weirder still, it changed colour from dark blonde to a burnt orange. It looked as if it had been scorched. The hair stylists at TVNZ couldn't get over how much the quality of my hair had changed.

These physical changes were a stark reminder of the strength of these drugs and I couldn't help freaking out about what was being pumped into my body. It was keeping me alive, but at what cost?

It was definitely the emotional impact that was the hardest to cope with. Rohan had warned me about the anger, mood swings, anxiety and depression. He knew what I did for a job and was concerned the drugs might have an impact on how I behaved on air. He urged me to take it slowly and not over-commit when it came to planning my return.

And yet I craved normality. It had been so long since I had had a routine or anything resembling a normal family life. I was so sick of being sick.

One thing that really helped was when Rohan put me in touch with a wonderful woman named Dr Galia BarHava-Monteith, another of his Churg-Strauss patients. There aren't many others with the disease in New Zealand and Galia quickly became an angel for me. A psychologist, leader and educator with an award-winning PhD to her name, this incredible woman inspired me with her experience and advice.

She had been along a very similar path, and seeing her now so full of life and energy filled me with hope. She also helped me in ways that doctors could not because, unlike them, she knew exactly what this felt like. We met up several times and I messaged her a lot with questions about the treatment and side effects. Galia became a source of enormous comfort, giving me the strength to believe that I, too, would make it.

I don't think I had realised how alone I had been feeling until I finally had someone who truly understood what I was going through. She would give me suggestions on how to cope when my medication was getting the better of me, and encouraged me to go easy on myself. We're still in touch today, and I feel so extremely lucky to have her in my life.

Stay back,
she's dangerous!

I n September 2015, four months after I got sick, I made the decision to go back to work. I knew I wasn't going to survive moping around at home much longer. If I were to have any chance of regaining my sanity, I had to return to *Seven Sharp* and get back to some kind of normal routine.

I also needed something else to focus on other than the illness. It wasn't just the time-consuming appointments and blood tests and treatments; I needed a distraction from my own thoughts and fears. It was time.

I was still having the monthly infusions, but the good news was that my inflammation levels were decreasing and Rohan felt I was on the right track. I was no longer in the 'life-threatening' category of Churg-Strauss, the nerve pain was under control and it was just the steroid side effects causing me grief now. Mackenzie was also completely settled. She had a great routine, and I'd still be able to spend the day with her until almost 3 p.m. when I would start my *Seven Sharp* shift.

So I went to see my boss at TVNZ, Pete Cronshaw, and told him I was ready to come back. Like Matt and Mum, who were both convinced it was too soon, Pete was concerned. The last thing he wanted was for me to relapse because of taking on too much. I was adamant I could manage. I told him I felt stronger than I had in months and convinced him that returning to work would be a good thing. I probably downplayed the impact of the steroids, but I promised him that if I wasn't coping, or if my health went downhill, I would immediately talk to him. I meant it.

Pete was amazing and said they would do whatever it took to make it work. Pippa Wetzell had been filling in for me while I was on maternity leave, so I always knew she would be there if I really needed her, too. I would work 3 p.m. to 7.30 p.m. Monday to Friday It felt more than doable.

Luckily we still had our amazing nanny, Sharon, who had been part of our lives since Juliette was little. She would step up her hours again, and Matt would be home from work by late afternoon to do the bedtime shift. I knew we could make it work, and for the first time in ages I was excited.

Healthwise, I wasn't 100 per cent, I knew that, but it helped so much that I was returning to a job I knew, with people I trusted and loved. The *Seven Sharp* team was like a family to me, and I couldn't wait to rejoin Mike behind the desk. He's one of this country's most controversial broadcasters, but he's one of the best workmates I've ever had.

It's years now since I last worked with him, but people still ask me what he's like. There is such a fascination around him. Maybe they think I'll dish some dirt on him, or spill some secrets, or tell stories about how horrible he was to work with. But there's genuinely nothing negative to say. Did we agree on everything? Absolutely not. Was he a diva? Not in the slightest. Did he have expensive taste in wine and an eclectic selection of men's fragrances? Yes, much to my amusement. But he was always super-professional and easy to be around. If I really wanted to do a particular interview he would always let me have it, and he made me laugh every single day. I thoroughly enjoyed working alongside him.

We would have feisty debates on and off air. I would find his black-and-white stances on things infuriating at times. 'Life isn't always that simple! It's complex and grey!' I would say when we were debating topics of the day.

One of the reasons we worked so well together was that we didn't compete. He had his strong opinions, but he always respected that I had mine, too. Television can be a cut-throat industry, with the few top jobs fiercely fought over. Mike and I were having fun, we both knew we were lucky to be the current choices, and we would enjoy it while it lasted.

On-screen chemistry between the hosts is so important on a show like *Seven Sharp*, and we were lucky there, too. It's not something that can be manufactured: either you gel or you don't, and we did. Our different styles balanced each other out. But the thing I loved most about working with Mike was knowing he always had my back. In live broadcasting you are hugely reliant on your co-host to work with you to make a successful show. Neither of us was easily offended, and we loved nothing more than taking the mickey out of each other.

So knowing I would be sitting next to Mike on my return to work made such a difference, and I couldn't wait to pick up where we had left off.

When Mike heard I was coming back I remember he sent me a lovely message, which was a great confidence boost for a fragile and sick new mum. 'Best news I've had in ages,' he wrote. 'Can't wait to have you back, Streety.' His wife, Kate

Hawkesby, also sent meals, baking and prezzies for the kids, which were very much appreciated.

In a planning meeting with Mike a week before I was due back on air, I told him about the steroid side effects and warned him there was a chance I might be edgy or I might handle things differently to the way I had before. In typical Mike fashion, he thought the idea of me flipping out on air was absolutely hilarious, and from then on anyone who came near my desk would be issued with a warning about 'Streety's roid rage'. 'Stay back, she's dangerous!' he would laugh. This was exactly what I needed — some light relief! It felt so good being back with colleagues, using my brain again, and talking about work stuff rather than my bloody health. It was the best distraction.

I could not have had a better boss than Pete Cronshaw. He let me work flexible hours, understood that I still had millions of medical appointments to attend, and even had meals sent to my house for my first week back at work.

The first day back on air felt amazing. I stepped into that studio, took my place on the *Seven Sharp* desk and breathed a massive sigh of relief. It felt like I was closing the door on a ghastly episode and stepping back into the life I loved.

If I wasn't worried about coping with my job, I did feel anxious that I was making my autoimmune disease look easy. For 30 minutes, five evenings a week, I was on screen smiling, laughing and smothered in makeup that made me look glowing and healthy. But it was a mammoth effort to get to that point. Some days I'd be in the makeup chair for much longer than my allotted time, pouring with sweat while the long-suffering girls in the makeup department tried every different foundation and powder in the hope it wouldn't slide straight off. They would often have to blowdry my hair halfway through because of my regular hot flushes.

Clifton Piper, the TVNZ stylist, had a tricky job, too, because I had gone from a size twelve to a very puffy size sixteen. Fortunately we still had my maternity outfits, so I stayed in those for quite a few months while I was having the steroid infusions. Then there was my hair — or lack of it. Thank goodness for fake hair pieces, which were pinned in each night to disguise the thinning patches.

The whole process of getting me ready to go on air was a masterclass in coverup. But as much as we tried, there was no disguising the weight gain and I was self-conscious about my puffy face. After my first week or two back there were some emails and Facebook messages from people asking why I had put on so much weight and why my face was so puffy. Several viewers asked if I was pregnant again and one thoughtful person helpfully suggested I should lay off the pies.

Mike's response to criticism from viewers has always been: 'Why do you care? Do you know these people? Why do you care what people who don't know you think of you?'

Of course it really didn't matter what anyone thought of me, other than the people I loved. 'Let it glide over you,' he told me. 'Don't take things too personally.'

The advice helped, and I tried not to let it get to me, but I still felt vulnerable and self-conscious. After a couple of weeks I decided the best way to deal with it was to speak out about my illness on *Seven Sharp* and explain why I looked the way I did. How could I expect people to be understanding if they didn't know what I had been going through? I was nervous about sharing my story, because I never want to be thought of as self-pitying, but I hoped my experience might help others who might be battling something similar, and also explain that I wasn't in fact pregnant for a third time.

The response was amazing — I received so many emails and letters and cards wishing me well and suggesting supplements I could take to help my symptoms. I was blown away. The most amazing thing, though, was hearing from others with long-term chronic conditions, and people who knew only too well the horrors of steroid side effects. Wow — there are so many of us going through this, yet because it's a largely invisible illness you can feel as if you're the only one in the world.

It really helped me when others could relate to the puffy

face and the weight gain. It made me feel it wasn't something only I was going through. Others had it, too, and I would come out the other side just like they had. It was really comforting. I was actually a normal person.

Now when I talk to others with a chronic illness there's an immediate level of understanding between us about each other's life. The exhausting reality of weekly blood tests, endless medical appointments and the rollercoaster quest to find out what's actually wrong. The amount of emotional energy consumed is hard to comprehend unless you have lived with it. It takes personal experience to understand never being able to properly relax because part of your brain is always fixating on how awful you feel, how can you fix it, and how can you find answers. It's relentless, and exhausting.

Being in the public eye has its downside but I've never regretted being open and sharing my story. I'm naturally a very open and honest person. If I ever did anything wrong as a kid I found it really hard hiding it from Mum and Dad! I was much more likely to confess in a flood of tears. I've lost count of the number of newspaper and women's magazine interviews I've done — nothing has ever been a 'no go' zone. I've shared my wedding, my babies and everything in between. And now, on my radio show *Coast Breakfast*, every single day I share anecdotes from my life outside work.

I know there are others in similar positions who go out of their way to safeguard their privacy and would never dream of sharing their family in the media, but I'm just not like that. I have always understood that having a public job means people are interested in my private life, too, and that's fine. It probably helps that I'm not harbouring dirty secrets or leading a double life. I'm way too boring for that. If people want to read about my new puppy or hear about my kids' funny exploits I am more than happy to share. I'm flattered that people are interested.

My approach to social media is similar. I try to share a mixture of work and home stuff, but I've made sure I haven't become a slave to it. When I wrote on Instagram about the steroid bloating I had messages from people from all around the country within minutes, sharing their own stories. They told me they too had piled on 10 kilograms in just a few weeks and were gutted about it. Pretty much everyone who had experience with steroids seemed to have a similar story, and in that moment it made me feel so much better. It was hugely comforting to hear from other people that it doesn't last forever. I had been googling like crazy but there is no substitute for hearing stories from real people telling me I wasn't alone.

I don't know if it's always wise, but I do sometimes engage with people who message me. I have learnt so much through my chats with others, especially about autoimmune conditions. None of my real-life friends have had the experience, but online I've built up something of a support network and it's been incredibly helpful for us all. We check in with each other and share experiences and advice.

Another thing I learnt through my illness was that specialists are a mixed bag. You'll hit it off with some, while others will fall well short of your expectations. I had been getting increasingly worried about my insane hunger and weight gain so was referred to a dietitian. I think I just needed reassurance that this was a normal side effect of the drugs and that at some point things would get better. I also hoped I would be given advice on healthy food choices to get me through the hunger pangs. But the dietitian's response knocked me for six.

'No one forces you to eat.'

'Pardon?' I said.

'No one forces you to eat,' she repeated. 'There are choices involved, even when you're on steroids.'

I felt like I had been punched in the guts. That one throwaway comment made me feel that any side effects I was having were completely within my control and I just needed to harden up. Get some willpower and I'd be fine.

I was in such a fragile place, still extremely unwell, and what I really needed was a kind approach from this health professional. I was just after some reassurance that what I was feeling was normal; I certainly didn't expect to feel shamed.

In dealing with any serious illness you need to find specialists and doctors you can relate to and feel comfortable with. Medical professionals who actually help you. If you're sitting in front of someone who is the opposite, you have a right to seek a second opinion, or speak your mind. I didn't have the energy to argue, so I just left and never went back.

Left to deal with the weight thing on my own, I decided I had to find a way to reintroduce exercise into my life. Training had always been part of who I am, and I knew I needed to get back to it — for both my mental and physical wellbeing. But my early attempts did not go well. A twenty-minute jog left me broken for days, and an attempt at a bootcamp nearly wiped me out.

It's probably no thanks to my background in competitive sport, but gentle exercise has always been a foreign concept to me. I quickly realised, though, that I couldn't dive straight back into the high-intensity training I loved. I had to listen to my body, so I started with walks around the block and eventually built up my strength to walk for longer and more often. Slow and steady wins the race.

Being back at work gave me a new positive focus and somehow I managed to hold it all together, never letting the steroid effects become too obvious, especially when I was on air. But there's no doubt it was exhausting juggling two little kids, my recovery and a full-time job, and on weekends I would collapse in a heap. I was still battling nerve pain down my back, especially when I was tired, and it usually struck at night. Matt would try to help with a back rub, but often even the lightest touch was painful. So I would throw back some painkillers and try to focus on the fact that at least it wasn't as bad as before.

I was definitely feeling more like my old self than I had in a long time. The kids were thriving and I was loving every second of being part of their lives again — going to special days at crèche and kindy, doing the morning drop-offs. Even having the energy to do a pretty hairstyle was a joy for me. The little things mattered, and made me feel like I was doing my mum job the way I had always wanted to. Every time I took them for a walk around the block or to the beach, or got down on the floor to do a puzzle with them, I was fully aware that I was lucky to have the chance.

When you have contemplated the possibility of not being there at all, every tiny moment with your kids feels amplified. It still happens sometimes. I'll be doing something entirely normal, like picking them up from school or watching a tennis lesson from the sideline and I'll be overcome with gratitude that I have this opportunity. That we're all still here and healthy.

When I got to the end of the infusions after six months it felt like a milestone, but it didn't mean the end of the steroids. I continued taking 20 mg a day for another six months, at which point I was allowed to slowly reduce the dose. It wasn't until I got down to about 10 mg that I started to feel like my old self — after almost two years. The mania subsided, my thoughts were clearer and I started to get my weight under control. The most exciting change was seeing the puffiness disappear from my face. Gradually I realised I could see my eyes properly again when I looked in the mirror. I would not miss that moon face! Even my wobbly middle was feeling a bit less wobbly.

I am now officially in remission from Churg-Strauss Syndrome, but I still take a small amount of medication and have to be on the lookout for signs of flare-ups in my body. I know when I'm overdoing it because my body sends me signals. My hands get covered in eczema or my asthma flares up and I know something is out of whack.

I have also had to learn to live life at a slower pace. I always used to think that sitting down doing nothing was a bad thing. I had to be constantly busy, doing something, going somewhere. Now, though, I have learnt to sit down and watch Netflix without feeling guilty, and I have learnt the importance of rest. It has taken me a long time to realise it's okay to do nothing.

My big goal is to get off all medication, but my specialist

says I'm not there yet. There is a strong possibility my disease will flare up again to the point I'll have to have the steroid infusions again one day. Until then I keep taking 3 mg of prednisone daily for maintenance. It does worry me to have been on steroids for five years, but I'm told I'll probably have to continue for the rest of my life. I'll happily do so if it means avoiding going back to that dark place.

Just as I thought life was back on track, I got a phone call from Rohan out of the blue telling me my weekly blood test had showed an unexpected problem with my liver. He was worried and wanted to see me immediately.

It was with a crashing sense of déjà vu that Matt and I went to hear Rohan explain there had been a huge spike in the marker for liver function, which suggested the Churg-Strauss was back and attacking my liver. If it continued, he explained, I would need a biopsy, and chemotherapy would likely follow.

I couldn't believe it. There I was thinking I was through the worst — and now this. It didn't make sense because I was feeling better than I had in ages and I thought the infusions were doing their job. I was a month or so back at work and that was going well, we had settled into a nice little family routine and I was so sure we had a lid on this disease. This was an unexpected and demoralising development.

Then Rohan raised the question of my fertility. He knew we wanted more children, and told us there was a high chance chemotherapy would leave me infertile. If we wanted to be sure, we should consider IVF. Creating and banking some embryos out of Matt's sperm and my eggs would give us an insurance policy for the future. The thought of undergoing further medical procedures didn't exactly thrill me, but it sounded as if it might be a case of now or never.

The timing wasn't great. We were due to fly to Noosa with my parents for a much-needed holiday to celebrate the end of the steroid infusions, but clearly my body had other ideas so we delayed the holiday and fast-tracked some IVF treatment.

To prepare for the egg-harvesting procedure I had to inject myself several times a day for a week or so prior. I was well used to needles by this point so that side of the process wasn't an issue for me, and I was fortunate I didn't notice any side effects, probably because I was already on so many other drugs.

On the day of the IVF, I was given a mild sedative, my legs were put up in stirrups, and the doctor at Fertility Associates extracted my eggs from my ovaries. This was done with a long probe of some kind, and while it's not something I would want to repeat too often, it was bearable. Matt was sent off to a little room for his part of the deal, and then it was a matter of waiting.

After a couple of days we were told that, despite my low

egg supply, three healthy embryos had been created. They were promptly popped into the Fertility Associates' freezer and we were able to relax in the knowledge that if I did need chemotherapy, at least our chances of having another baby weren't ruined. We were so lucky.

In the midst of all this my blood results miraculously settled again. It was the night before I was due to get the liver biopsy and my specialist rang to say it seemed I no longer needed it. She was baffled by the results, but it meant I had dodged the chemotherapy (again!). It was a massive relief but the rollercoaster ride of ups and downs was frustrating. I was struggling to understand what was going on inside my body, and we still have no idea what caused the liver results to spike. Who knew what the future held?

We jumped on a plane to Noosa the minute the treatment was done, three days later than initially planned, and it felt so good to finally escape and have a chance to celebrate getting past those awful infusions. At last we could take a deep breath, sit back and just have a bloody good rest. My parents could relax again now that I wasn't at death's door, and Juju and Mickey were so excited to be in Australia on holiday. Mum and Dad looked after the kids a lot so that Matt and I could enjoy being a couple again. It felt like so long since we had been able to do normal things like hang out at the beach and go out for dinner together. I felt better than I had in months.

Sophie, my surrogate

One of the things Matt and I shared from the start of our relationship was the desire to be parents. Even as nineteen-year-olds we were not too shy to admit we wanted kids, and lots of them. When we finally got together, we would lie around having rambling, dreamy conversations about what our future might look like, and it always involved a little tribe. We wanted three or four children, and both agreed we wouldn't leave it too late in case we had trouble getting pregnant.

I always knew that children would be a gift not only for me but also for my parents. Having Juju and Mickey gave them a whole new lease on life; a renewed sense of meaning and purpose. They still make the four-hour drive up to see them at least once a month, they call most days to check in, and there hasn't been a birthday party or performance where my parents haven't been there. If Matt and I need a night off, they're there in a flash, the long drive no barrier; there's just no keeping Nana and Grandad away.

As the girls grew up out of toddlerhood, we knew we wanted to add to our family. It was a matter of when, not if. My body had taken a hammering so it was so comforting knowing we had three embryos on ice if we ran into problems. If it turned out my egg supply was shot, at least we had those to rely on.

Around six months later I found myself thinking all the time about having a third child. It's hard to describe how it feels when you know you're not done. I felt like our family wasn't quite complete. Matt was far more wary, worried about the stress another pregnancy would put on my body. By this stage I was still on prednisone, but managing the side effects pretty well.

Mum was in Matt's camp, worried about the impact another baby would have on my health. I remember having a few feisty discussions with the pair of them about why they were so down on the idea of me wanting another baby.

The only way to settle this was to get a medical opinion from my now trusted ally, Rohan Ameratunga. We made an appointment and I bustled in there with Matt to find out when we could start trying for another baby.

Rohan looked at me as if I was crazy.

'I don't think that is a good idea. It's far too much of a risk.'

He explained that in Churg-Strauss patients, the body's autoimmune reaction gets more and more severe with each pregnancy. I had seen that myself — with Juliette it was the severe reaction I had after taking the Voltaren and Nurofen together, not to mention the big flare-ups of asthma and eczema. With Mackenzie it was organ failure.

'It's a risk you absolutely cannot take,' said Rohan, spelling out very clearly that a third pregnancy could kill me. 'Maybe you could look into surrogacy,' he said.

I was devastated. All along, I believed that my health would settle and I'd eventually be well enough to have another baby. I so wanted a big family. When I think back now, I must have sounded slightly delusional. I don't know what part of me thought I could handle another episode like the medical drama I had after Mackenzie was born. I knew that post-pregnancy my body had flipped out, but I wanted a third baby so badly I had somehow made myself believe I would be fine. I was fixated.

As for Rohan's suggestion of surrogacy: I didn't know a single person who had done it. It was something people in Hollywood did; it certainly wasn't something I would ever entertain.

I struggled to accept that I could not carry another baby. With both Juliette and Mackenzie I'd had really good pregnancies. Getting pregnant and being pregnant had been straightforward, and their births had not been an issue either. It was what happened afterwards . . .

There had to be a way around this. Perhaps Rohan was being over-cautious?

I arranged to meet the one person I knew might have faced this same dilemma and would understand my plight: Galia, my Churg-Strauss friend.

I told her I was desperate to have another baby and asked her what she thought.

Her face said it all. 'You can't do it, Toni,' she said. 'You simply can't risk it.'

It wasn't what I wanted to hear.

My specialist, parents, husband and trusted friend were all in agreement: there was no way I could risk getting pregnant ever again.

Matt was unequivocal. He would love another child, but no way in hell would he let me risk my life for it.

It's hard to explain how I was feeling. Even though my mind understood the reality, my heart just couldn't accept it. My need for another baby was almost a physical ache. Over the next few weeks it began messing with my mind and grew into an obsession. I would look at my girls, who I loved so much, and instead of feeling content I would think 'They need another sibling.' I would see families with three kids and get hit by a pang of sadness and envy.

All my life I had imagined myself with a big family, and I know it sounds crazy but two children just didn't feel right to me. It wasn't enough.

At the same time, I felt guilty for having these thoughts. Why couldn't I be happy with the two beautiful children I had? There were so many people out there who could not have even one baby. I felt like I was being greedy.

It was a tumultuous time mentally. I probably seemed fine on the outside but these thoughts were occupying my every waking moment. It got to the point where the urge for another child was with me constantly; the more I tried to suppress it, the more intense it became. I was so stressed out.

As crazy as it sounds, I was able to visualise my third child. He was a boy and he was beautiful. He had olive skin and brown eyes and I already loved him in that indescribable way you love your children. I saw myself holding that baby; I could almost smell him. I felt a genuine connection to a baby who did not even exist. But I just knew I had to find a way to get to him. All my hopes were hanging on advances in medical science. Maybe there was some medication I could take to stop my immune system from going haywire next time? I needed an urgent cure for Churg-Strauss Syndrome, basically.

By this stage I was not only hosting *Seven Sharp* but had also taken on a second job — co-hosting *The Hits Breakfast* radio show with Sarah Gandy and Sam Wallace. I hadn't gone looking for another job, but when it was offered I couldn't say no. I had always wanted to try radio, and here I was getting the chance to host a breakfast show with two people I really liked. The bosses were happy to work around *Seven Sharp* and my family commitments. How could I turn that down?

The fact that my old mate Sam would be my co-host was a massive part of the appeal. Mike Hosking was making it work with his Newstalk ZB job in the mornings and *Seven Sharp* at night, so I didn't see why I couldn't handle it, too.

I knew working at both ends of the day would be tough, and my life already felt pretty full, but I took the role and gave it my all.

The priority was to make sure the girls wouldn't suffer, so

Matt and I decided the only way to make this work was if he quit his job to be a stay at home dad. So that's what he did.

While the girls were little, the schedule actually worked pretty well. My alarm went off at 4.30 each morning. I would sneak out of the house and Matt would get the girls ready on the days they had crèche and kindy. I usually got home around 11 a.m. and was able to do the lunchtime pick-ups. I would hang out with them until it was time to head in to *Seven Sharp* at about 3 p.m. I probably saw more of my children than if I had been working a nine-to-five job, even if it meant I got pretty tired.

Having two jobs was intense, and in the long run unsustainable, but I made it work for a year by having a very disciplined routine. I very quickly learnt that if I wasn't in bed asleep by about 8.30 p.m. I was ruined for the following day. That meant my social life pretty much died. This wasn't a huge change, though, because having two kids had already proved enough of a handbrake! It wasn't like I was turning down invitations all the time. Despite being exhausted, I felt incredibly lucky to have two jobs I loved.

This super-busy period also helped keep my mind off the baby disappointment. I talked to my family and close friends about it at length, and even saw a counsellor to help get my head around it. It made me really sad, but I was starting to accept that my family of four was complete.

I was enjoying a quiet glass of wine with Sophie during a weekend in New Plymouth when she casually dropped a bombshell. 'I'd like to be your surrogate.'

Um, excuse me? One minute we were catching up on kids and work, the next she was offering up her uterus. Sophie has always been the most loyal friend, but even for her this was next level. I laughed it off, telling her she was the best friend a girl could ever dream of, but I would never allow anyone to go through that for me.

'I'm serious,' she insisted. 'I want to do it.'

She must have had too many pinots, I thought.

Again, I told her not to be silly; there was no way it could happen. Sophie had just been made CEO of a large Taranaki law firm, her kids were still young, and her life was insanely busy. There was no way she could fit another pregnancy into her world.

'You have enough going on,' I laughed, before kissing her goodbye and heading back to my parents' place. Not for a moment did I take Sophie's offer seriously, but I was really touched by the gesture.

In the morning I woke to a text message: *I'm serious about what I said last night. I want to do this for you and I want you to let me.*

Again, I thanked her for being the world's best friend but brushed off the offer. It was far too huge to contemplate seriously. Over the next few days the messages continued.

Please let me help you. I am 100 per cent serious about this.

Let's just investigate the process and see what happens.

I picked up the phone and called her.

'Soph, this is a very big deal — you can't just decide this. I bet you haven't even spoken to Mike yet'.

'Oh, I haven't talked to him, no,' she admitted.

(Oh my god, she hadn't even run this insane idea past her husband? What on earth would he say?!)

To be honest, at this point I didn't even know how I felt about someone else carrying my baby, let alone the extreme burden I would be putting on my bestie and her entire family.

I love my friend, but man she can be stubborn. When Sophie sets her sights on something, nothing gets in her way. It's a remarkable personality trait that has served her extremely well over the years.

'I'm not giving it any more thought until you've talked to Mike,' I told her gently.

In the meantime, I tried to go about my days with this weird scenario floating through my head. Surrogacy? How reliable is it? How does it even work? Why would Soph even suggest this?

A couple of days later she called again, this time to tell me that Mike was on board.

'*What*?!' I said. 'You're seriously telling me he's relaxed about the idea of you being pregnant with someone else's baby?'

'There's no one else he would like to help more,' she said. 'He's totally supportive.'

I started to cry, and Sophie's voice was wavering, too. She told me she had spent enough years feeling helpless in the face of my struggles — after Stephen died, and again when I was ill with Churg-Strauss — and now she had finally found something she could do to help. Surrogacy, she said, was something she wanted to do for me and my family.

'It's actually a pretty simple thing to do,' she insisted. 'We're talking about a year out of my life — it's not a big deal.'

I was overwhelmed. It hit me that this was all coming from a place of love for me and my family. Most friends would bake a lasagne but Soph was offering up her womb.

I was still finding the offer hard to deal with, though. I hate being a burden and I hate putting people out — how could I possibly contemplate another person carrying a baby for me for nine months? It was too much.

At Sophie's insistence, however, I agreed to do a bit of research into how surrogacy works in New Zealand. I cautiously started googling. There was very little information and it was clearly a pretty complicated process, but just reading about a couple of Kiwis for whom it had worked well planted a tiny seed of hope. There are about 60 babies born via surrogacy each year in New Zealand . . . maybe my baby dream wasn't over after all?

Was I seriously considering this?

The next few weeks were a bit strange. Sophie, Mike, Matt and I were carrying this amazing little secret and, even though none of us dared to believe it might amount to anything, just having the idea bubbling away felt kind of exciting. But we agreed there wasn't much point talking about it further until we had all the information, so I launched a fact-finding mission and made an appointment with Dr Mary Birdsall at Fertility Associates.

Mary didn't seem surprised to see me. I had completed one round of IVF with her and she had expected me back to explore my options at some stage.

She told me that while a surrogacy arrangement between Sophie and me was, in theory, entirely possible, it was important we understood the magnitude of such an undertaking. In her easy-to-understand way she explained the process from start to finish, and the truth is that I went away from that meeting with a sinking feeling that this was too big a mountain to climb. I couldn't ask Sophie to jump through the many, many hoops that were necessary to make it happen.

I was surprised to learn that there is no specific surrogacy law in New Zealand. The process is dealt with under the Adoption Act 1955 and the Human Assisted Reproductive Technology Act 2004. I didn't know it at the time, but I was to become a bit of an expert on both over the coming months.

Mary wasn't trying to put me off; she just wanted to make sure I knew that the surrogacy process is long, complicated and emotionally challenging for everyone involved and wasn't to be undertaken lightly. Every surrogacy arrangement in New

Zealand requires the surrogate and intending parents to receive approval from ECART (the Ethics Committee on Assisted Reproductive Technology). For that, they need medical testing, individual and group counselling, legal assessments and consultations with Oranga Tamariki, the Ministry for Children, and this whole process can take up to a year. Only then can fertility treatment begin — if you get approval.

After the birth, the intending parents need to adopt their child from the surrogate, even if she has no biological connection to the baby, as would be the case with us. That part really blew my mind. How could Sophie and Mike be the legal parents of a baby that was 100 per cent biologically mine and Matt's? I guess I could understand Sophie's role in it as the birth mother, but Mike? The idea that he, theoretically of course, could claim a legal right to our baby seemed completely insane, and an unnecessary additional burden on him and his family.

Mary also explained that New Zealand's surrogacy system is altruistic, meaning a surrogate cannot be financially compensated. While we could pay for things such as medical costs and things relating to the pregnancy, a surrogate cannot legally be reimbursed for time off work, or receive any other kind of gratuity or payment.

It seemed to me that there were very few protections in place for either the surrogate or the intending parents, so I asked Mary what would happen if Sophie decided she didn't want to hand over the baby to us at birth. It was a hypothetical question of course I never in a million years feared that would happen. Mary said we would likely end up in court and there was no guarantee that we would win.

It was dawning on me what a massive deal this was. The level of trust and goodwill required between the parties was huge. And nine months is a long time during which the unpredictable could happen. What if, for example, we changed our minds halfway through? Sophie and Mike would be left with full legal responsibility for a baby that wasn't biologically theirs.

The more I found out, the more obvious it became that surrogacy is definitely not for the faint-hearted. I couldn't even begin to understand how scary it must be for people making such an arrangement with someone they didn't know well. Sophie and I had a twenty-year friendship behind us, and throughout the entire process I never lost sight of how lucky we were. We trusted each other implicitly.

I was grateful for the information but more than a little dejected and overwhelmed when I left the hour-long appointment at Fertility Associates. I had no idea that surrogacy would be such a complicated process. The statistics also made for grim reading — in New Zealand only 30–40 per cent of IVF treatments result in a successful pregnancy, and miscarriage is more likely with IVF conceptions. The odds were against us.

I emailed Sophie and Mike with everything I had learnt and fully expected they might have second thoughts. This was an awful lot to commit to. It just seemed too massive an undertaking to contemplate. I made it very clear that Matt and I would fully understand.

'Well, that all sounds pretty straightforward,' Sophie replied in an email. 'Let's take the next steps.'

Sophie's guts and determination have never failed to amaze me, but the fact that she wasn't put off by all this left me gobsmacked. She is such a pragmatic thinker; she read the information, applied it to our situation and felt confident we could do it. Matt and I are so lucky to have this woman in our lives. There are not many people with a big enough heart and the mental strength to take on something like this.

We needed to get together, the four of us, to really talk things over. Soph and Mike were due to come up to Auckland from New Plymouth, so we set up a time for what we jokingly named the 'surrogacy summit'. We hadn't let anyone else in on our secret yet, so it was all rather cloak and dagger. They flew up on a Friday afternoon, leaving their kids, Bella and Theo, at home with their grandparents.

The first part of the evening was pretty much like any other time they've come to stay. Juju and Mickey were thrilled to see their Aunty Willow and Uncle Mike, and we had an early dinner. Once the kids were in bed, we convened in the living room for 'the summit' and the mood quickly changed.

For the first time in the history of our friendship, things felt kind of awkward. This was such a big thing. There was a tension in the air and none of us quite knew how to start. I still felt uncomfortable, particularly in relation to Mike. I was afraid he might think I had coerced or persuaded Sophie into it, or that he was only lending his support because he had a very determined wife.

Eventually Matt cut to the chase. 'Right, let's talk about this.'

I cleared my throat, battling an urge to cry, and told Sophie and Mike that the most important thing I wanted to get across was that they absolutely did not have to do this for us. I thanked them for being so kind and selfless, but I needed Mike to know he had the right to speak truthfully about how he felt about it. I had known Mike nearly as long as I'd known Sophie, and I was confident I could accurately assess how he was feeling if he spoke honestly about his concerns. I needed him to speak up if he felt the impact on his family or the risks for Sophie were too great.

I couldn't bear the thought of him agreeing to go ahead against his better judgement, just to make Sophie happy. The emotions that night were so intense; the enormity of what we were contemplating was impossible to ignore. It felt momentous — an evening none of us would ever forget.

When Mike spoke, what he said blew me away. He told us he had thought about it all a great deal and that we had his full support. We were the only people on earth he would consider doing this for, but he and Sophie both wanted to go through with this because they knew how much another baby would mean for our family. They had talked through all the risks, and they were confident she could physically handle another pregnancy. His lingering worries were only for Bella and Theo, because he didn't want them feeling confused, embarrassed or left out.

The impact on Bella and Theo worried me, too. So for the next hour we discussed the impact on our children and agreed that the only way forward was total honesty. If we spoke openly to them (and others) about what we were doing, without shame or judgement, we would normalise it for them. If kids at school asked questions or made comments, they would at least be armed with all the information and be able to respond confidently.

Sophie is someone who has always lived her life the way she wants to. She's not fragile and doesn't obsess about what others might think of her, and that made it all so much easier for all of us. She said we should feel proud about what we were doing.

I was at pains to make Sophie and Mike understand that they could change their minds at any point in the process. I didn't want them to worry that our friendship might suffer if they decided against continuing. Because it genuinely wouldn't have. I felt they had done enough just coming this far with us.

We talked about so many things that night, and by the end of the evening we had agreed to take the next steps. It was about midnight by the time we collapsed into bed. I was exhausted but I couldn't get to sleep because my mind was running at a million miles an hour.

Until now I hadn't allowed myself to believe we might actually get a baby out of this. Now there was a glimmer of hope and it felt unreal.

Praying for a miracle

Matt and I went back to Fertility Associates to officially start the surrogacy process. The clinic would manage the application for us, which was a relief because the amount of paperwork involved was huge. We hired a family lawyer with experience in reproductive law, Zandra Wackenier, and she quickly became an integral person for us, helping us navigate the legal requirements and answering all our questions that cropped up along the way.

Lots of criteria had to be met in order to obtain ECART approval, including proving that I was unable to carry a baby myself and that Sophie had finished her own family. Those were the easy bits — a letter from Rohan made it clear another pregnancy would endanger my life, and Mike's vasectomy several years earlier showed he and Soph did not want any more children. They were absolutely content as a family of four.

The success of our application would be heavily dependent on the outcome of several counselling sessions. Over a couple of months the four of us (Sophie and Mike, Matt and I) attended many hours of often intense sessions. Essentially, we had to convince the counsellor that we were all emotionally stable enough to cope with the process. We had individual counselling, couples sessions and appointments with all four of us together. No stone was left unturned — with the counsellor's guidance we discussed every possible eventuality. If a surrogacy arrangement goes wrong, it goes spectacularly wrong, we were told, so it was in everyone's best interests to prepare as thoroughly as possible. We needed to ensure we were all on the same page before we took any further steps.

The ethics committee needed to know how we would react to various different scenarios. What would happen if Sophie changed her mind partway through? What if she wanted to keep the baby once it was born? What if Matt and I changed our minds or if something happened to us during the pregnancy? Who would raise the baby if we died or were incapacitated?

We also had to discuss what we would do if complications emerged. What choices would we make if abnormalities were discovered during scans? Would decisions be made by me or Sophie? Did we have the same views if termination was an option? Some of the scenarios were upsetting — what if Sophie were diagnosed with cancer, would we terminate the pregnancy so that she could have treatment? Every potential scenario had to be discussed because, as Zandra continually stressed, these were all things that had happened in real-life surrogacies. She told us about a heart-breaking situation where a surrogate mother took her own life while carrying a couple's baby because she couldn't cope with the enormity of what was ahead of her. It was a stark reminder of how big a deal this was, particularly for Sophie. Every time we discussed something of this magnitude it made me feel slightly ill that these risks were only a reality because of me.

We also had to decide how we planned to make our (hypothetical, at that stage) baby aware of his or her story. Everyone has the right to know where they come from, so we had to show we had discussed and made a plan for this. Again, I just felt so lucky that we were doing this with Sophie. She was such a big part of our life, a special aunty to our girls already, and our best friend, so it was pretty easy to show that we planned for her to remain in our lives forever. The fact that our baby grew in her tummy would never be a secret; it would be forever celebrated.

It was exhaustive and exhausting, but I can see why the counselling is a crucial part of the process. We had to be aligned in our thinking. We had to eyeball each other to make sure this was really what everyone wanted. It was particularly demanding for Sophie, who had to fly up to Auckland from New Plymouth for each session. While we of course paid for her flights, the surrogacy rules meant we were not allowed to reimburse her for time off work so she had to use her annual leave. The rules were the rules and we weren't about to jeopardise our application by breaking them. But it did seem wrong that we couldn't at least pay Sophie for her lost earnings.

The counsellors found Sophie, Mike, Matt and me to be remarkably aligned in our thinking. This didn't surprise us, but I think the counsellors were pretty amazed. There was nothing that needed follow-up discussion because we were in agreement on all the big stuff, and that was hugely comforting. We knew we were approaching the surrogacy with a shared understanding and total mutual trust. Again, I felt so lucky to be doing this with my lifelong friend. I already knew what she would say to the counsellors when they asked her a question — it was like asking myself.

One surprising thing about the counselling process was how deeply it delved into Matt's and my marriage. The ethics committee apparently needed a clear picture about how we dealt with stress as a couple and how we resolved our differences. They had to be sure that we were up to the challenge, I guess. At this point, I felt really grateful to be in a strong marriage in which we are pretty united on our approaches in life. We're not afraid of the odd barney if we disagree, but fundamentally our values are the same and we've always approached life as a team. One of the questions on the form was 'How do you resolve conflict?' I jokingly said I'd put down 'We argue until Matt realises I'm right!' I'm sure that would have gone down brilliantly with the committee!

On top of the physical and emotional considerations of surrogacy there are also the financial implications. It was going to cost more than we had expected.

We had had three embryos stored with Fertility Associates when we thought I'd be going through chemotherapy. Devastatingly, they were no longer viable. New research had been published linking the immunosuppressant drug mycophenolate to birth defects and miscarriage. I was on that medication when my eggs were harvested, and it meant those precious little embryos were now unusable. We were gutted; it felt like we'd gone through IVF for no reason, not to mention that $15,000 was now down the drain.

The all-up cost of the surrogacy was about $50,000. The

biggest part of that was the two rounds of IVF, at about $15,000 each, with legal and medical fees making up the rest. I know how privileged we were to be in a position to do it, and I'll always be so grateful that our income gave us the freedom to pursue our dream. The truth is, though, that Matt and I probably would have sold our house and all our possessions to get there if we had needed to.

Because we had agreed from the start that we would be open and honest about how we were feeling, I often told Sophie how guilty I felt that I was putting her through this. She would just reassure me every time. She was adamant — this was entirely her decision and I needed to ditch those feelings. 'I understand the risks, I understand the impact on my life and I'm going into this with my eyes wide open,' she said. 'I want to do this for you. Let me do this for you.'

It was time to share our secret with the people closest to us. I knew my parents would be emotional, but the news left them speechless. Dad was over the moon and just astounded by what Sophie was prepared to do for us. Mum was a bit more circumspect. She was happy for us but worried about Sophie, and I discovered later she phoned Sophie and asked if she could come and visit.

They both eventually told me about this meeting. Apparently Mum walked in the door and they hugged and both burst into tears. Sophie told Mum she was doing it for all of us, not just me, and she said she hoped it would go some way towards making up for the pain of losing Stephen. Mum had always loved Sophie; this was a new level of appreciation entirely.

I was nervous about what Sophie's parents would think. They would have been well within their rights to be angry at me for even thinking about putting their daughter through something like this. I fully expected them to freak out about the impact on their grandchildren. I felt sick about it, to be honest, and I told Sophie that.

Soph was confident they would come on board in the end and she was right. They were shocked initially — understandably. Karen and Martin's main worries were the health risks for Sophie, and the effect on Bella and Theo. But after a lot of questions and discussion they realised their daughter had made up her mind and they accepted it. They, like the rest of us, knew that when Soph set her mind on something, she usually made it happen.

Sophie assured me they were on board and supportive, but I needed to talk to Karen myself. I took a deep breath and dialled her number. I had to hear first-hand that she wasn't angry with me and that she understood why we were doing this.

Karen conceded that she was worried about Sophie and the kids, but she trusted her daughter to make good decisions.

She had faith that Sophie would have done the necessary research and knew what she was doing.

'We're with you all the way,' she told me. 'And we're incredibly proud of Sophie.'

Karen and I had a little cry about what an amazing person Sophie was for doing such an incredible thing, and I began to feel so much better. It was only after that conversation that I allowed myself to believe that this might actually happen. All the people who really mattered were now part of the process and I could relax a bit.

As part of the approval process, we had to select two people to act as referees — people who knew us well and could vouch for us, to confirm that our intentions to have a child were honourable and legitimate.

Sophie and I agreed that along with my mum, our mutual friend Vanessa Biddles would be the ideal person. We'd known her since university, she was part of our tight little circle of friends and she was amazing with secrets. But she was also cautious, conservative and risk-averse. Unlike Soph and I, who have been known to be a tiny bit spontaneous, Ness would think things through methodically before leaping in.

'You're *what?*' she said, when we told her what we were planning. 'Oh my god. This is big.'

Yep, it was big, but by this stage we felt totally confident we knew what we were doing. We now just needed Ness on board.

And after talking with us for hours and hours about the ins and outs of it all, Vanessa said she thought it was an incredible thing and she was honoured to be part of the process. We had her 100 per cent support.

She promised she would be by our sides every step of the way. We didn't know it then, but Ness would turn out to be a crucial player in our surrogacy journey.

As part of the ethics approval, we had to begin a formal adoption process. It seemed bizarre given that Sophie wasn't even pregnant yet, but social workers from Oranga Tamariki visited Matt and me at home to assess our suitability. They were perfectly lovely people, and made the process as easy as they could, but I was struck by the ridiculousness of the situation. No one had checked us out when I was pregnant with the girls, so why was it necessary now when any new baby would also be our biological child?

It felt like such a waste of valuable time and resources when they could have been helping families who actually needed it. It felt like a total farce that people have to legally adopt their own biological child. After several visits our household was deemed to be a safe place to bring in a new baby, and Matt and I were given the all-clear too.

The fact that the Adoption Act dates back to 1955 is proof enough that it needs updating. Back then, no one could have imagined modern-day fertility treatments, let alone a surrogacy involving implanted embryos that have no biological link to the birth mother. I soon found there were many others out there — doctors, lawyers and parents — who were just as frustrated by the process as we all were.

It took a good six months to get through the counselling, legal appointments and form-filling before our application was ready. It felt momentous sending it off to the ethics committee, but we were all careful not to over-celebrate, even though it felt like we had made a pretty solid case.

We went back to our normal lives and tried to put the application out of our minds. Keeping busy wasn't hard — I was still working two jobs. I loved them both, but when Juliette started school in October 2017 I found working nights really tough. I no longer saw her when I got home in the middle of the day, I had gone to work by the time school finished at 3 p.m., and she was asleep when I got home at night. This was not the sort of mother I wanted to be.

I spent months agonising over what to do, but in the end the answer was obvious. Did I want to ever see my daughter? Of course there was no question. I loved *Seven Sharp* so much and I know people thought I was crazy when I stopped, but something had to give. I simply couldn't have a job that meant I was absent from my kids' lives. I talked the decision over with a counsellor, and this gave me clarity and confidence that I was making the right personal call for me and my family. I talked to Mike Hosking, who totally supported my decision (and ultimately followed me out the door), and also my executive producer, who totally understood. We agreed I would stay on until December, and announce my departure then.

I hated the thought of leaving because it was my dream job and I was totally happy there, but the moment I made the decision I felt a huge weight lift off my shoulders. I hadn't realised how much the thought of not seeing Juliette was stressing me out until finally I did what I had known all along I had to do. That experience taught me that if something isn't working for you and your family, you have to find the courage to change it. You have to listen to your gut so you don't have regrets. I was worried I had ruined my TV career, but I should have had more faith — in both myself and my employers.

It was a couple months before we heard anything back from ECART about our application. Of course I had moments of stressing about what we would do if we got turned down, but Matt, always the rationalist, would say, 'There is no reason for them to turn us down.' Sophie and I adopted a mantra right at the very beginning: 'If this is meant to be, it will be.'

We just had to be patient. Finally, many months after our first foray down this path, an email arrived with the news we had all been hoping for — the application had been successful and we were approved for surrogacy.

It was a big moment, but I didn't feel as jubilant as I had thought I would. I knew this was just the first step — there were many more hurdles to come. I also felt that familiar rush of guilt about Sophie again. What if she felt she couldn't back out now that it was approved? I had to reassure her and Mike that they could still change their minds.

I understand if you can't go through with it. Please don't feel like you can't tell me, I texted her, soon after the approval was granted. *I will be okay. Our friendship is more important.*

Shut up! Sophie replied in her trademark style. *We've got approval, let's get on with it!*

Now the legal side was sorted, it was time to embark on the medical side. This meant another round of IVF to try to create some viable embryos. I had my usual anxieties — what if I didn't have enough eggs? The first time we did this they said my egg supply was low, and since then I had been through a major illness, had two surgeries, and six months of steroid infusions and taking other serious medications. My body had been through the mill.

Like the first time around, I had to inject myself every day for a week with a hormone treatment to stimulate my ovaries and encourage egg production. The more eggs, the more chances we would have to create healthy embryos, so everything was riding on it.

Most women in their early thirties like me have well

over 30 eggs, but it turned out I only had ten. It wasn't the best start — and things got worse. We were crushed to learn that we managed to get only one embryo from the process. One! I couldn't believe it. This meant we had *one chance* at this surrogacy — if the embryo didn't take, and Sophie didn't fall pregnant, we would be right back at the start. I realised I hadn't prepared myself for this at all.

This was an unwelcome reality-check for Matt and me. Everything had gone so well up to now, but our chances were looking slim. I called Soph with the news. Unlike me, she decided to view it positively.

'It's one embryo and it's healthy and perfect and it's going to work. I can just feel it.'

God, I love this woman. Her positivity was incredible and I knew she was right — I needed to have some faith. From then on, I tried to focus all my energy on being positive.

While I had been having eggs harvested, Sophie had been preparing her body for the implantation. She was also taking hormone medication, and was having regular blood tests to monitor her cycle so that the embryo could be implanted at the optimum time.

It was early December 2017 when the embryo transfer day finally arrived. Sophie and I had it all planned — she would fly to Auckland around noon, I would collect her from the airport and we'd drive straight to the Fertility Associates clinic in Ellerslie. We would arrive in good time to relax and channel positive energy and good vibes into this one shot at a miracle. Or so we thought.

But when Sophie woke up that morning, New Plymouth was blanketed in a thick fog and all flights in and out were cancelled. She called me straight away and we both panicked for a bit. That little embryo was already thawing and we only had a small window to make it work. As I got on the phone to the clinic to see what our options were, Sophie drove to the airport just in case.

Just as we were working out whether she had enough time to drive to Auckland, there was better news. The fog briefly lifted and Soph managed to talk her way onto the only flight out of New Plymouth that day. The relief!

She was due to land at 4.30 p.m. and the doctor agreed to stay late to get the transfer done. We were *so* grateful. There was no point in me battling rush-hour traffic to collect her, so I headed to the clinic while Sophie jumped in a cab from the airport.

It was such a relief when I saw her taxi pull up, but we barely had time for a hug. We had to get in and get this done.

Hilariously, the lovely specialist who had agreed to stay late was also dealing with his own family logistics. He had had to pick up his son from daycare and bring him back to work with him to get our procedure done. The little boy wasn't too happy about this. He just wanted hang out with his dad, and he bawled when he realised that wasn't going to happen. I felt bad about that.

All gowned-up, Soph hopped up on the bed and I sat at her side. All the while we could hear the boy's sobs as the poor receptionist tried to distract him. It wasn't quite the peaceful and serene experience we had envisaged, but it was definitely memorable. For such a miraculous procedure it all felt fairly routine. In the space of about five minutes the embryo was transferred into Sophie's womb, and all we could do now was wait and hope.

It would be ten days before we knew if the transfer had resulted in a pregnancy, and as we left, a nurse asked who they should call with the news, Sophie or me. I immediately said it should be Soph, because it concerned her body, but she was adamant that Matt and I should be the first to find out. 'It's your baby, not mine. You just ring me with the news.'

Sophie returned to New Plymouth the next day, while I tried my best to pretend I was relaxed about the whole business. I knew I should have been preparing myself for the worst, but I'm a true believer in the power of positive thinking so I went with that. The odds were against us: only a 40 per cent chance of the embryo taking. Even though I hadn't said this out loud, I had decided that if this didn't work I would not ask Sophie to go through it again. I would take it as a sign that it wasn't meant to be.

I had a few conversations with Soph that week, and we couldn't help but nervously chat about whether she was already pregnant or not. One of us would say something like: 'I know we're not meant to say this, but I have a feeling this is going to work out.'

Rightly or wrongly, we were both willing this to be a success.

Oh, boy!

The morning after I announced on air my decision to leave *Seven Sharp* I received a phone call from an unknown number. I was tired: it had been an emotional night, and I was out doing some errands with the kids.

I answered the phone.

'Hello?'

It was a nurse from Fertility Associates. Oh my god, this was it. This was the call. I had to sit down. 'Are you there?' the nurse asked. 'Yes, I'm here,' I whispered.

'I'm calling to let you know the transfer was successful. Sophie is pregnant.'

I had not allowed myself to think this far ahead, but here we were — Sophie was pregnant with our baby. The surrogacy process I had never allowed myself to believe in was actually happening. I had to call Matt. I didn't know where he was, but I had to get hold of him.

'Sophie's pregnant!' I yelled down the phone.

We both rushed home and we just looked at each other in disbelief, smiles spread wide across our faces. It was really happening! We couldn't believe our single little embryo had taken. We had to tell Sophie. I called her phone but she didn't answer, so I sent her a text. *Call me, we have news.*

A few seconds later my phone rang and it was her — she had ducked out from a work lunch and was talking in hushed tones. 'OMG have you had the call?' she whispered.

'Yes — you're pregnant!' I blurted out through tears. 'You're pregnant!'

'I knew it!' Sophie said. 'I can't believe it; this is amazing. Wow, wow, *wow*!'

We then called my parents, who had a similarly emotional

reaction. Actually, Mum could barely speak through her tears. It all felt so unbelievable.

The next few days passed in a strange sort of euphoria. Every morning when I woke up, my mind would go to that little baby cooking away in my best friend's tummy and I felt a jittery sort of happiness settle over me. I was unbelievably excited, but at the same time I was still telling myself to stay cool. It was early days — Sophie was only four weeks' pregnant so we were by no means out of the woods yet. And we knew the miscarriage risk for IVF babies was higher.

But as each week went by with Sophie still pregnant, I slowly began to let myself believe in this miracle. I was so overwhelmed with gratitude for what Sophie was doing that I didn't have even a hint of sadness that my baby wasn't growing inside my own womb. That's not to say that feeling didn't come, because it did, but in those initial weeks all I was focused on was Sophie's pregnancy making it past the all-important twelve-week mark.

Sophie never complained, but I knew she was super-tired and battling morning sickness and I felt terrible about it. I tried to think of ways to both make it easier for her and to express my gratitude. I wanted her to know she was constantly in my thoughts so I texted and called often, but I didn't want to smother her either and I certainly didn't want her to think I was checking up on her. It was a balancing act. The law meant we couldn't pay her, but that didn't mean we couldn't send care packages, book her in for massages and arrange for meals to be delivered. It wasn't much, but I hope it made a bit of a difference.

Having our surrogate in another city meant there were a lot of logistics involved, and we had to line up medical care in both places. She signed up with her obstetrician in New Plymouth, the woman who had delivered Theo and Bella, and in Auckland she was overseen by Ammar, the wonderful specialist who looked after me when I had Juju and Mickey. They were happy to cooperate to make this thing work, and we were never made to feel that our situation was odd or weird.

I flew down for Sophie's first scan when she was about six weeks' pregnant. It was the first time I had seen her since the embryo transfer day and I hugged her so hard when she met me at the airport. Knowing she was carrying our precious little baby felt utterly surreal and I couldn't stop staring at her in awe. In hindsight, I was possibly a bit creepy!

The scan was an amazing experience. I sat next to Sophie in the darkened little room, holding her hand as the radiographer squirted the jelly and guided the scanning wand across her tummy. It's always nerve-racking waiting to hear the heartbeat, but seeing our tiny baby jumping around on the screen was the best feeling ever. Sophie lay there smiling while I wiped away tears. I flew home the next day feeling more grateful than I believed possible, and totally in awe of what we were part of.

Matt and I wanted a boy. I know you're not meant to have a preference, or if you do you shouldn't admit it. But the idea of having a son filled me with excitement. That's not because we already had two girls and fancied something different, or because of some weird masculinity complex on Matt's part; it was inextricably tied up with thoughts and memories of the people we had lost. On both sides of our family, boys were scarce. I had lost two brothers, my parents had lost two sons, and Matt had lost his dad. Of course a little girl would have been equally loved — and three daughters has a lovely feel to it — but I longed with all my heart for a son, and in a hard-to-explain kind of way it was all because of Stephen. I wanted the joy of a little boy back in my family's life.

So you can imagine our excitement when we found out that it was indeed a boy in Soph's tummy. She was only ten weeks' pregnant but in our over-cautious way we had paid for pre-natal blood testing to rule out chromosome disorders. The results showed our baby was a healthy little boy and we were over the moon.

I was hit with a strong sense that Stephen and Lance must have had a hand in this in some way. Mum felt the same, as though those two little boys were sending us a message. We were already so lucky to be in this position — and now we were also having a boy? I was sure when the specialist rang he was going to reveal it was a girl; I really thought he was joking to start with. The whole thing was hard to get my head around. I had a best friend willing to make a huge sacrifice, one embryo with terrible odds, and yet here we were, on the cusp of welcoming a son we thought we would never have. It felt miraculous.

It was starting to feel real, and I finally allowed myself to let go of the self-protective armour and embrace this amazing new chapter in our lives. Sophie came to Auckland for the twelve-week scan, and this time there were three of us in the room, Matt and I sitting on either side of Sophie, enthralled as our baby's image appeared on the screen. There he was, with his perfect little arms, perfect little legs and everything appearing to be in working order. We were so grateful.

Sophie was dealing with everything like a total boss. She was so diligent and so careful about ensuring he was safe as he grew inside her. She also made huge sacrifices for us: she gave up her beloved long-distance running, she didn't touch any of the foods that are off-limits for pregnant women, and she did everything absolutely by the book — no sneaky sips of wine for her.

She was much better than I would have been the third time around! She joked that she felt like she was being more careful with our little boy than she was with her own kids. It must be a strange thing carrying the responsibility of someone else's child, but she relished the challenge.

I tried to be at every scan with Sophie. Either she would

fly up or I would go down; we even did one scan via Facebook Messenger. Because I wasn't carrying my baby this time, I grabbed any chance to be part of the pregnancy process.

Once Sophie reached the twelve-week mark we shared the news with our children. Juju and Mickey were little, three and five, so I was pretty sure they would take it in their stride. We were all a bit more nervous about how Soph's kids would digest the news. The whole surrogacy thing is confusing enough for adults; how would children get their little minds around it?

Matt and I sat our girls down one afternoon and told them they were going to be big sisters. They were so excited and both immediately looked at my tummy, searching for evidence. 'You know how Mummy has been really sick? Well, the doctor said I can't grow another baby in my tummy so Aunty Willow is going to carry the baby in her tummy for us,' I told them.

They both stared blankly at me, processing the information for a few seconds, then replied 'Okay cool.' And that was that: they both accepted this very non-standard situation like it was the most normal thing in the world. They were stoked to be getting a baby brother and I remember them jumping around the room in excitement.

In New Plymouth, Sophie and Mike were having a similar conversation with Bella and Theo. They approached it in really simple terms, explaining that Aunty Tones and Uncle Matt were having another baby but it was growing in Mummy's tummy because my one didn't work well anymore. They tried to make Bella and Theo feel they were part of this amazing thing, too, telling them they could help make the baby happy by talking to him and singing to him while he grew. They told them they would always be very special people in this baby's life, but that their own family would not change. 'The baby will grow in my tummy, but I won't be the Mummy,' Sophie told them. 'I will only ever be your mum.'

She explained that when the baby was born she would give him to Matt and me and he would be Juju and Mickey's little brother. She told her children it was something to be proud of, and if their friends at school asked questions, they could just tell them what was happening.

Bella and Theo had a lot of questions, but Sophie and Mike were amazed by the way they seemed to accept it without judgement or fear. I remember us all commenting on how nice it would be if adults approached life in the same open-minded way.

With Sophie's pregnancy starting to show, we needed to work out how we would share our news beyond the family. New Plymouth is a small town and people were beginning to give Sophie sideways looks — especially those who knew Mike had had a vasectomy!

Juju and Mickey were busting to tell their friends that they were having a little brother, so we needed to make some decisions. Matt and I wanted Sophie to take the lead in deciding how much information we shared, when and with whom.

I was fairly relaxed about people wanting to know about me because of my very public job. But this was all new to Soph, and if she wanted to stay anonymous then we would do all we could to shield her. It turned out, though, that Sophie also wanted to be honest about the whole process. People were going to start asking questions about her growing belly, so keeping it all a secret wasn't really an option for any of us. Also, when I suddenly popped up with a third child, having had no pregnancy, naturally people would want to know how we suddenly had a son.

'Why keep it a secret when it's something we should all be proud of?' Soph said.

I was worried for her, though. I'd had years to get used to public criticism but I hated the thought of Sophie being a target. She shrugged it off. 'Who cares what people say? They don't even know us.' That's the pragmatic friend I know and love — and sometimes wish I could be more like!

That ability to ignore the haters can be incredibly helpful, and I remember thinking what a gift it must be to be so unburdened by anxiety about what other people think of you. It's something I'm yet to master . . .

We decided to announce our baby news on Instagram:

Exciting news for Matt, Juliette, Mackenzie and I . . . We're having a baby due in August! We're incredibly blessed to have my childhood friend Sophie Braggins carry our precious bundle for us, and to have the unwavering support of her husband Michael. My battle with the autoimmune disease Churg-Strauss means I can't carry another baby myself, so we're extremely lucky to have such a special and selfless friend offer to be a surrogate for us. #heartisfull #babyboy

As I uploaded the post, which was accompanied by a photo of a blue baby-sized Swanndri bib, I mentally prepared myself for the response. I was nervous some people might think I was greedy and selfish for putting my friend through a pregnancy when I already had two healthy children. Then there were those who might be against surrogacy in general. I knew it would be picked up by the media and I didn't want Sophie to have to deal with any trolls. There was no going back now, though. *Here we go!* I texted Sophie.

I put my phone down and went off to make a cup of tea, before returning for a nervous peek at the comments. I was amazed. My Instagram was absolutely flooded with messages of congratulations, my inbox was filling up, and *none* of it was mean or nasty. Sophie's Instagram page was the same. Every single person who took the time to write — and there were thousands of them — seemed genuinely thrilled for us. I was so relieved and so touched; why had I not had more faith in the world? This reaction confirmed to me that surrogacy is something special and joyous that should be celebrated. Ultimately, I was happiest for Sophie, who so deserved all the praise being heaped on her, because what greater gift is there than what she was doing for us?

We followed up the announcement with an interview with *The New Zealand Herald*, and I spoke openly about the surrogacy on *The Hits Breakfast*. It became obvious that there were *so many* people out there struggling to have babies — those who couldn't conceive at all, those who had one or two children but couldn't get pregnant again. It also highlighted a lack of knowledge around surrogacy. I had people asking me all sorts of questions: Where do you find a surrogate? How much does it cost? Who is eligible?

I was new to this whole process myself, but I tried to answer people's questions or put them in touch with appropriate experts who could. I distinctly remember one touching message I received from a high-profile Kiwi businesswoman. She said she had given up all hope of having a third child until she read our announcement, and it had given her a glimmer of hope that there might still be a chance.

I felt a growing sense of responsibility — Sophie and I could use our experience to encourage and educate others. I called Sophie. 'This could be really powerful,' I said. 'We can show people it's possible.'

One of the questions people most often ask me is how it felt to be having my baby grow in another woman's body. The answer is that most of the time it felt absolutely fine. I focused entirely on my gratitude for Sophie, because the alternative was no baby. I do think that it was made easier by having already carried two babies myself. I already knew what it was like, and knew how lucky I was in that. I hadn't missed out entirely. I suspect it would be harder if it was your first pregnancy.

But I would be lying if I said there were no moments of fear, longing or sadness. Sometimes during the pregnancy I felt I was missing out, and longed to feel his kicks inside my tummy as he grew.

I worried about whether we would bond when he arrived. Would he love me if he hadn't been carried by me? Would he be scared when he was taken from Sophie and given to me? Would he long for his birth mother? I also wondered about how much of a baby's personality was determined by what they experienced in utero.

I can't say I was sad about not being able to breastfeed the new baby. I accept that breastfeeding is the best start to life, but the reality is that lots of mums can't, for all sorts of reasons. I wasn't breastfed as a baby because my twin brother was battling leukaemia and I turned out fine. Some mothers are able to induce lactation after having a baby via surrogacy, but my Churg-Strauss meant I couldn't take the necessary drugs, so he would have to go straight on to a bottle. I had no concerns about formula — I knew he would thrive.

Any fears I had turned out to be unfounded, but at the time they were very real. I had the dream surrogacy arrangement, but these worries still crept in and I knew that only time would tell. For now, I just had to roll with this incredible journey, do my best to stay strong and positive, and keep reminding myself that it would all be worth it when we had our little man in our arms.

I have talked to other people whose babies have arrived via surrogacy, and they all agree that throughout the process there's always a tiny seed of fear in the back of your mind. The biggest one for many women is: What if the surrogate won't hand over my baby? For me that fear was non-existent because I knew that unless Sophie completely lost her mind she would never do that. But for those embarking on this process with someone they don't know well, I can imagine it's much harder. While most people who become surrogates are incredible humans with the biggest hearts, for the intending parents it must be nine months of extreme anxiety.

Mum was a great sounding-board in my irrational moments. She reminded me of the months I had spent with Nana when I was a baby and Lance got sick, and pointed out that it had had no impact on our bond. 'He'll know you're his mother,' she said, reassuringly. Mum was right, I needed to be calm and trust in the process.

I did have to make Matt understand at one point, about halfway through the pregnancy, that the whole 'not getting to carry my own baby' thing was sometimes tough for me. He was surprised — he genuinely hadn't thought about that aspect. I didn't want to pretend I was all blasé about it. Yes, I knew there was no other way for us to have a baby. But any woman who has been pregnant will know it's a very special time. Your baby bump serves as a constant reminder of how your family is about to change. With no baby bump, sometimes it felt like this baby wasn't even real and that scared me a bit.

Without the physical reminder of a pregnancy, it was quite easy to forget sometimes that we were about to welcome another child to the family. We could go for a few days without even talking about it at home, which is pretty weird really. In a normal pregnancy, everywhere you go people notice your baby bump, and ask how far along you are. Because I had been through it twice before I didn't miss this public aspect at all, and I was delighted Sophie was being made a fuss of wherever she went. Sophie said people reacted so beautifully when she told them she was carrying a baby for her friend.

We did try to be quite purposeful in preparing ourselves and the girls. We decorated the nursery early on and went shopping for baby boy clothes. We let the girls choose toys and presents for their little brother, and we would Facetime Sophie heaps to talk to the bump.

On the whole I didn't find the process of surrogacy

particularly emotionally difficult, so when I was hit with the odd wobble, it was quickly followed with a rush of 'oh my god, we're so lucky'. Matt and I were both very aware that without the surrogacy there would be no baby at all, and that would have been far tougher than the fact that my growing baby was being looked after by my best friend.

Army of Spiders

I headed into 2018 feeling so positive. Sophie's pregnancy was going brilliantly, my work–life balance had become manageable now that I had just the one job, and my health was great. In fact I felt better than I had in years. I still had regular blood tests to monitor my eosinophil levels and regular check-ups with Rohan, but I was officially in remission from Churg-Strauss. My daily steroid intake had been cut right back to a maintenance dose of 5 mg a day, at which level the side effects were barely noticeable most of the time.

So everything was looking good and we were just fizzing over the fact we were going to welcome our little boy into the family around the middle of August.

Then, in early April, things started to veer off course.

I had taken some time off radio to host the 2018 Commonwealth Games for TVNZ. The Games were held on Australia's Gold Coast, and I was the evening anchor in the Auckland studio. I was pumped because I love sport, and it was the chance to host a live event.

The weekend before the Games were due to start was Easter, and we spent it with Mum and Dad in New Plymouth. While I was there I developed a bit of a sore throat. I ignored it for a day or two, but when I started to lose my voice I knew I had to see a doctor, with the Games only days away from starting. I could hardly turn up to work with no voice, could I? I wasn't panicking, though — I had had laryngitis before and it always cleared up pretty quickly.

I made an appointment at my local medical practice. I explained I had to be on live TV the next night and so really needed to knock this thing on the head to ensure I had a voice. The doctor printed off a prescription for antibiotics and scnt me on my way. I got home, took the first two tablets and went to sleep, hopeful that I would be right by the morning.

When I woke up I took another two pills before heading into the studio for the first day of Games coverage. I always love going back to TVNZ — where I started my career and where I feel so at home. I skipped into hair and makeup, sat down and had my usual natter with the makeup team while they knocked me into shape, before heading to wardrobe to choose my outfit.

As always, there was a buzz about the place. Live TV is always exciting, but when we're covering a major event it's next level. Excitement and nerves are all bundled up together, but that's what I love about it. I was rostered to present live from 7.30 p.m. until about midnight, and for the first half of the shift I felt great. My voice was back, I had loads of energy and all was well. The antibiotics were clearly doing their job.

But halfway through something changed, and I started to feel really heady. I wasn't myself and I felt really low in energy, which was strange for me as I usually have good stamina. I put it down to this cold I had.

When I finally signed off at midnight I was so relieved. I drove straight home and flopped into bed. I woke the next morning feeling just as bad as the night before. Naturally, I didn't for a moment consider calling in sick. I don't do sick days, unless I'm on my deathbed. That's not something I'm proud of, by the way — there have been many times in my life when I have stubbornly ignored quite major issues for fear of putting others out. But there was absolutely no way I was going to call in sick, not when we were covering something as major as the Commonwealth Games.

I dragged myself in to work and plastered on my happy face for another day of live television. But as soon as I plonked myself down in the makeup chair, Lisa Matson, the makeup artist in charge of getting me glammed up that day, looked at me anxiously.

'Are you okay, Toni? Your eyes are a bit yellow.'

I leaned forward to look at myself up close in the mirror. She was right: the whites of my eyes did have a quite a yellow tinge.

I wasn't that worried, though. I had the Commonwealth Games to focus on, so I just put it to the back of my mind. Halfway through my shift I had another weird symptom: I started getting really itchy legs. As I had some tight leggings on, I just put it down to that.

I finished my shift and rolled into bed again.

In the morning I woke up and told Matt that Lisa had thought I had a yellow tinge to the whites of my eyes. He looked at me and agreed.

A quick google said it was likely I was suffering from jaundice, which can be caused by all manner of things, including hepatitis, gallstones or tumours. None sounded ideal — or very likely.

We wracked our brains for clues as to what could have

brought this on, and the only thing I had done differently was starting that course of antibiotics. I decided then and there to stop taking them in case, and the next morning I went straight back to the GP.

'You've certainly got a bit of jaundice,' he said. He sent me for a blood test and suggested I consult Rohan, my Churg-Strauss specialist, in case it was autoimmune-related.

Over the next few days I experienced a whole raft of bizarre symptoms, none of which I felt were bad enough to stop me from fronting the Commonwealth Games coverage. My throat came right, but I started to have bouts of nausea. I felt as if I had run a marathon, the itchiness would come and go, and the yellowness had started spreading across my body.

I was determined to finish the Games coverage. Matt was grumpy with me but I remained resolute — it was only ten days. And who else could step in at such short notice? I had been preparing for this for months, I knew all the events and the athletes, and I would not let the team down. There was no option but to ride it out.

I kept up the façade for the next six days, giving it my absolute all when I was on air, then collapsing in a heap the moment I got home at night. By the time my appointment with Rohan came around my entire body had a slight yellow tinge and he was immediately concerned.

'Oh, Toni. This isn't good.' He was his usual caring self — he pulled out his Dictaphone and started talking into it, as he always does — 'yellow skin, yellow eyes, antibiotics, severe reaction' — before telling me it was clear my liver wasn't functioning properly. He strongly suspected the antibiotics had something to do with it and referred me to a liver specialist, Dr Rachael Harry. I felt so gutted.

Like Rohan, Rachael also suspected a reaction to the antibiotics. Her first step was to test my bilirubin levels. Bilirubin is a yellowish pigment made during the normal breakdown of red blood cells. In a healthy body it passes through the liver and is excreted, but my liver wasn't processing the bilirubin properly and that's what was causing my eyes and skin to turn yellow.

My blood test results were shocking. A normal bilirubin level is less than 25; mine was 118. 'You have a serious liver injury,' Rachael said, adding that it was lucky I stopped taking the antibiotics when I did. There was no clear reason why my body had reacted in this way, and nothing to suggest I was prescribed an incorrect antibiotic — this was just the reality of living with Churg-Strauss: for some unknown reason I had developed an allergy to erythromycin, the antibiotic I'd been taking for laryngitis.

I couldn't believe this was happening. My mind went straight to my baby, who was due in just a few short months. I could *not* get sick again. I simply had to be well before August. I felt like crying; I just didn't have the energy to go through something like this again.

'What's the treatment for a liver injury?' I asked, wondering if it would mean more steroids or worse — chemotherapy. 'There is no treatment,' she said. 'It's a matter of waiting and watching.'

No treatment? That couldn't be right. Rachael explained I had to have daily blood tests at Auckland Hospital to monitor the bilirubin levels. It would get worse before it got better. The hope was that my liver would begin to heal and the bilirubin levels would decrease.

'But what if they don't?' I asked.

'Then you'll be looking at a liver transplant.'

A *transplant*? I couldn't believe what I was hearing.

How on earth could taking an antibiotic lead to a liver transplant? It felt like an all-too-familiar nightmare was returning.

The next few days were a blur as I tried to process what was happening. Matt was his usual amazing self, switching straight into crisis mode and promising me that we would get through it together, just like last time. My parents came up from New Plymouth and moved in, ready to do whatever they could to help, as per.

My health was deteriorating by the day, so I called my Hits radio boss, Todd Campbell, and told him I needed some time off.

'I should be better in a week or so,' I said optimistically. It would end up being closer to two months.

The bilirubin began invading every part of my body. It was different to the Churg-Strauss pain from my previous health crisis. This time I was nauseous, my joints ached and I was lethargic to the point of barely being able to move. The cruelty of a liver disease is that you can't take painkillers because they can cause further damage, so the only thing I had was anti-nausea pills, which barely made an ounce of difference.

The itching started to ramp up. I know it doesn't sound like much, but it grew to become the hardest thing of all to deal with. I've had eczema for most of my adult life so I know what it's like to be insanely itchy, but this was different. It was unbelievable — I was itchier than I had ever thought possible, and it soon took over every waking moment. My arms, stomach and legs were the worst.

I tried to be gentle, but at times I became so desperate I'd scratch until I bled. I itched in my sleep, and would often wake to find my sheets dotted in blood and my skin scratched raw. My dear, patient dad would sit with me for hours, gently scratching my legs and trying to keep me from despairing completely.

The only way to describe the feeling is that it was like I had an army of spiders marching around under my skin. It was a diabolical sensation and it was driving me insane.

I discovered from my specialist that the itching is a common side effect of liver disease, caused by the high levels of bilirubin trapped under the skin. Until those levels came down it would continue. There was nothing I could put on my skin to calm the itching. All they could give me was a disgusting grainy yellow drink called Colestid, which binds bile acids in the intestine and has been shown to help some patients with the itching. I don't think it made any difference, but I kept taking it just in case. I even went to a hypnotherapist, but the itching continued.

My days were eerily similar to when I was sick with Churg-Strauss — the couch became my home and I lay there for weeks in my PJs, feeling weak and miserable, relegated to being an observer of family life again. Juju and Mickey would come and go for cuddles, bring me their toys and their drawings from school and kindy, but I had minimal energy to engage with them. I felt utterly hopeless. I was so unwell I could barely watch TV or scroll through my phone; I just stared into space. Yellow skin, yellow eyes, nauseous and itchy. So. Insanely. Itchy.

And I couldn't stop thinking about Sophie in New Plymouth, who by that stage was seven months' pregnant with our baby boy. I just had to get well in time for him. I felt so angry that my health was failing at a time when the focus should have been on Sophie and the baby. Instead, my family's lives were on hold because my body was letting me down again. It was depressing.

Every day I had to drag myself off the couch and into the car for a blood test at Auckland Hospital. It was a two-hour round trip, which pretty much used all the strength I had. The yellowness had flooded my system from top to bottom, and the blood tests kept showing the bilirubin levels increasing.

Which meant the itching continued to worsen. My mental state was getting wobblier by the day, so Mum took me back to see Rachael, the liver specialist, and sat there with tears running down her cheeks as I suggested the doctor put me in an induced coma. I hadn't slept for more than an hour or two at a time in weeks, my skin was scratched raw and I was done. I was losing the will to live, I told her.

Rachael was sympathetic. She had seen this level of itchiness before and the desperation it brings. She told me about a big, burly policeman she had treated in the UK who had opted for a liver transplant purely to stop the itching. That made me feel a bit better — if he was driven to those extreme measures, perhaps my despair was understandable.

Rachael explained that putting me into a coma wasn't an option, but urged me to hang in there, saying it usually came right in seven to twelve weeks. I know that was supposed to give me hope, but I burst into tears. I had endured four weeks, and the thought of another eight sounded like a life sentence. The prospect was unthinkable.

The people around me were struggling, too. Mum was scared — a few times I'd seen her crying when she didn't think I was watching. She was amazing with the kids, but whenever she looked at me I saw the frightened look in her eyes. I could also hear the many hushed conversations she had with Matt, Dad and my sister. I felt so guilty for putting her through this. She didn't need this stress — she should have been at home in New Plymouth pottering in the garden or seeing her friends. You know, normal stuff that retired people do, not stuck up here running around after her adult child.

My radio bosses were so supportive, but I started to stress about the impact on work. I couldn't believe how long it was taking to get better. My co-hosts, Sarah Gandy and Sam Wallace, both came to visit and I got quite teary when I saw them. Lots of my incredible friends left baking and meals at the door, or popped in for five minutes, but I was genuinely too sick for visitors.

One of my besties, Ness, decided that maybe a trip to the beach for some fresh air would help lift my spirits. She was running a café at the time and had brought my favourite chicken sandwiches. She drove us to the beach, and I dragged myself out of the car and onto a park bench overlooking the sea. I took one bite of the sandwich and tears started to roll down my face. I so wanted to enjoy this moment, but neither the view, nor the sandwich — not even my friend's company — could make me feel any better. I was a total misery-guts. The eternal optimist was no longer hopeful.

Every day the specialist would call with more bad news. 'Still no improvement,' she would say apologetically, as if my blood test results were somehow her fault. Day after day for weeks on end my bilirubin levels continued to rise. Rachel usually called with the results in the afternoons and I would cling to my phone, willing the results to be good for once. I clearly recall the dejection I felt when my bilirubin reached 227 (remembering that under 25 is normal). I desperately searched for signs of improvement within myself, but there was nothing. I felt worse than ever and the itching got even more intense.

It was a waiting game, and while you're waiting you start to fear the worst. 'I'm going to be one of those patients that doesn't improve after twelve weeks, I'm going to need the transplant,' I convinced myself. Then I'd go down the rabbit hole of what that would mean. Months, possibly years of recovery — how would I look after a new baby?

Sophie flew up from New Plymouth to visit in the hope it would lift my spirits. She knew I was ill, but when she walked in and saw the state of me she burst into tears. I was completely yellow from head to toe, drawn in the face and could hardly get up off the sofa. Everyone wanted to help, but there was absolutely nothing anyone could do. We just had to wait and pray that those bilirubin levels would start to fall.

Seeing Sophie with her beautiful big baby bump was bittersweet. It was so lovely to see, but at the same time it amplified my fear and guilt. I had reached the point where I thought I was never going to get better, and it must have been daunting for Sophie to see the mother of the baby in her tummy in such a state.

After eight weeks, totally out of the blue, I got the news of a slight drop in my bilirubin levels. I didn't care that it was a minuscule decrease; this was all I needed. Rachael tried to keep my expectations low, explaining that we needed a run of good results before we could celebrate. But the next day brought news of another slight drop.

I was jubilant. I still felt like death, but for the first time since this sorry mess began I started to believe I might actually get better. From there, apart from a couple of devastating days when my bilirubin results shot up again, a downward trend was established. And amazingly, I started to feel better. As quickly as the symptoms came on, they began to subside.

The first thing to improve was the itching — hallelujah! The nausea then lessened and my energy started to increase. After about ten days I was almost back to my old self. I had been to hell, but I was on my way back. My body had done its job, my liver had recovered and a transplant was now off the table.

It amazes me, looking back, how quickly I recovered once the bilirubin started decreasing, and I was so happy to be up and running again. It was like after my previous illness: normality was bliss. Even boring things like cooking the girls' dinner or washing their hair in the bath filled me with joy.

I remained yellow for months after but I didn't care, and I

practically skipped into work on my first day back at The Hits.

The biggest joy of course was knowing I would be fully fit to look after our little boy, whose creation had been the result of so much loving effort by so many of us. I just couldn't wait to meet him.

The most
amazing gift

'**A**re you at all scared your surrogate might want to
keep the baby once it's born?'

I was asked this question so many times
throughout Sophie's pregnancy that I came to realise there
is a real feeling of suspicion and mistrust around surrogacy.

Not around our arrangement in particular, but the process generally. There is so little information about it and a shroud of secrecy that sees so few surrogacy stories told publicly.

I got the distinct impression that people thought I must be living in fear that Sophie would go on the run with our baby once he was born. To be fair, our archaic law governing surrogacy makes that possibility very real. In the past year there have been a couple of disastrous surrogacy stories in New Zealand that support that fear, and I was heartbroken for the families involved.

The surrogate mother faces the same level of risk under current law. What if I, as the intending mother, suddenly decided I didn't want the baby? By law, that would mean Sophie and Mike remained the legal parents.

All the counselling for our ethics application was tough, but it absolutely did the job in ensuring we were confident about each other's intentions. The whole point of the process was to make sure Sophie was mentally sound and emotionally strong enough for the daunting task that lay ahead. In fact it turned out she had the perfect temperament for surrogacy. Even though we viewed her actions as extraordinary and miraculous, she saw her role as a straightforward one.

'I'm growing this baby because I can and you can't. It's not actually very complicated,' she said. As far as she was concerned, this was another challenge she had set herself, and she was determined to do it well. In fact she often told us she felt privileged to be part of something so special. 'Most people don't get the chance to experience something like this but I'm right in the centre of it. I'm the lucky one.'

It's also really important to remember that Sophie did *not* want another baby of her own. She and Mike had finished their family, which is why he had had a vasectomy after Theo was born. They were done with nappies and sleepless nights, and I know that towards the end of the pregnancy Sophie was seriously counting down to the time her life could return to normal. She couldn't wait to get back into her normal clothes, be able to run around with the kids again and enjoy a couple of glasses of wine. Nine months is a long time to give your body over to someone else's child.

That's not to say Soph didn't form an attachment to the little baby growing inside her. She did. Like any pregnant woman, she felt a warm reassurance with his movements and kicks, and her growing baby bump became part of her family. Theo and Bella would chat to her tummy, and Sophie often rested her hand on the bump in that protective pregnant-lady way. She was really connected to this baby; I wouldn't have wanted it any other way. Her feelings for him were never those of a mother — she viewed him as an extension of me and my family.

As perfect as Sophie was for the task, there were a number of times in the process when it occurred to me that perhaps *I* wasn't entirely cut out for it, because I continued to struggle with guilt over what I was inflicting on my best friend. The pregnancy was a huge disruption to her life, and at times I felt absolutely sick about it.

I worked myself up over how I could lessen the load for her, how on earth we could repay her, whether I could find the right way to say thank you. Which of course was a waste of time because there is *nothing* adequate that you can do to repay someone who gives you a child.

I had to work hard to accept Sophie's gesture for the extraordinary gift that it was. It was given out of love, it's as simple as that. Sophie knew how I felt, she knew we were grateful, and I so wish I had been able to accept that earlier and let go of the guilt.

The due date — 17 August — was fast approaching. Carrying someone else's baby is one thing, but giving birth to a child you don't get to keep is an entirely different challenge. I've had two babies naturally; I know where labour takes you emotionally and physically. It's agonising, it's scary and it can take forever, but all that is forgotten in a heartbeat when your baby is placed in your arms at the end.

Sophie wouldn't have that. She would be handing the baby over to us. How on earth would that be for her? I knew she'd be happy for us, but what would the physical and emotional toll on her be?

Another fear lurking at the back of my mind was what if something went wrong? There are risks attached to any birth, and I would never forgive myself if Sophie didn't come through it well. Looking back, I was more worried about Sophie than the baby. I never once worried about our baby boy — I always felt a calm confidence that he was going to be just fine.

It was up to Sophie to decide how she would give birth to our baby. If she wanted a home birth we would have supported her. If she had wanted to have this baby alone in a forest we probably would have agreed (but I'm glad she didn't). We wanted her to know she had full control when it came to the labour and birth. It was our baby, yes, but it was her body, and this was absolutely her decision.

If she had wanted us nowhere near the birth we would have respected that, but all along Sophie was adamant Matt and I should be there.

'You're his parents — he needs to see you first,' she said.

While she had given birth naturally to Bella and Theo, Sophie decided on an elective caesarean section. It was important to her that she differentiate between the experiences of birthing her own children and the way she was having ours, and she felt that a surgical birth would be more controlled and clinical, and less emotional for us all. We completely understood where she was coming from.

It also made sense logistically — we could book in a date that suited us all, and Sophie could plan her return to normal life around it.

There are strict guidelines around caesarean sections in New Zealand, though — you can't just choose a surgical birth because you want one, even if you're under private obstetric care as we were. You have to be able to show that it is required for medical or psychological reasons. Medically speaking, Sophie didn't need a caesarean, but we believed there were genuine reasons from a psychological perspective. With the support of our obstetrician we wrote to the district health board explaining our reasons and, thankfully, approval was granted. I think it was fairly clear that Sophie needed to be able to choose what she felt would be best for her emotional recovery.

In consultation with both obstetricians we booked the caesarean in for 14 August at North Shore Hospital. We planned it meticulously. Sophie and Mike would fly up to Auckland the day before, and the three of us would be at Sophie's side for what we hoped would be a calm, stress-free delivery. With Sophie's encouragement I reserved a room at Birthcare, a postnatal facility in Parnell, where Matt and I would go with our baby for a couple of days to focus on the bonding process. Mike would stay with Sophie while she recovered in hospital.

Several days before she was due to give birth Sophie flew to Auckland for a final appointment with the obstetrician and for our baby shower lunch, which we thought would be a lovely celebration of this special time and everyone who had helped get us to that point.

Sophie arrived on a Thursday and spent the night with Matt and the girls because, in a case of poor timing, I had to stay the night in a showhome for a radio promotion. It was my last day of work before maternity leave, and my co-hosts and I were broadcasting from an empty house in a new subdivision in Hobsonville Point.

I was so excited to get that final day of work done, knowing Soph was waiting for me and our baby would soon be here. I raced straight home after the show, collected Soph and we headed to Ponsonby to meet Ammar, our well-dressed obstetrician, at a café to discuss our birth plan. I love how casual he was — he just wanted an informal chat about the birth, so there was no need to do it in his clinic. Trendy Ponsonby was far more his style.

It was wonderful to see Sophie! She was *so* pregnant, and it suddenly hit me how close we were to meeting our baby. I hugged her tightly and held her there with my little boy squeezed in between us. 'Not long now,' Sophie said, and I was overwhelmed with excitement.

We ordered our smoothies and were soon joined by Ammar, who all along had made no secret of the fact that he loved being part of our surrogacy journey. It was one out of the box, he said.

'How are you feeling?' he asked Sophie, his voice full of professional concern as he sat down. She told him she was fine, but he didn't seem convinced. 'Are you sure?'

Sophie admitted that she'd had a restless night's sleep at our house and had a bit of an upset tummy that morning.

'Don't drink that!' he suddenly said, ordering her to put down her smoothie. 'We need to go straight to the clinic.'

Ammar told us he wanted to check for early signs of labour, because to him, Sophie just didn't look quite right. I hadn't noticed a thing, but apparently she had discomfort written all over her face. It just goes to show how attuned doctors can be to their patients.

As Sophie and I made the ten-minute drive over the harbour bridge to his clinic across the road from North Shore Hospital, she started having mild cramps. When we arrived at the clinic Ammar wrapped the monitor around her tummy and the lines on the screen said it all — every few minutes the graph would rocket, clearly showing that Sophie was having regular contractions. She was in labour! We listened in disbelief as Ammar told us the baby would need to be delivered in the next couple of hours. If we risked waiting, the labour would progress to the point where it would be too late for a caesarean.

It was 9 August and the caesarean had been booked for the fourteenth.

Mike was in New Plymouth and this was absolutely not how it was meant to be happening. We grabbed our phones. Sophie told Mike he needed to get on the first plane out, and I rang Matt and barked orders down the phone. 'It's all go!' I told him. 'Grab our overnight bags and meet us at North Shore Hospital asap!'

Then I phoned my parents, who also headed straight to the airport; our nanny Kate, who rushed to the house to look after the girls; and my sister Kirsty, who packed a bag and drove straight to Auckland from her boyfriend's place in Tauranga.

Sophie and I were trying fairly unsuccessfully to stay calm. We were both fizzing with excitement and anticipation, but also worried about whether Mike would make it in time. Then he called back to say there were no flights that would get him here soon enough.

Sophie's contractions were ramping up and we knew we couldn't hold off on the operation much longer — this baby wanted out.

I made the snap decision that I would step into Mike's shoes and be Sophie's support person, while Matt focused on the baby. It wasn't ideal, but I wasn't going to leave Sophie on her own after the caesarean. I knew our baby would be fine with Matt until Mike arrived to take over from me.

But Sophie wasn't having it. 'Call Ness,' she said. We hadn't planned to have our friend Vanessa at the birth, but in that moment we both knew she would be the perfect support person. She'd had a caesarean herself, she was one of our closest friends, knew everything about our surrogacy journey thus far, lived nearby, and was great in a crisis.

'I'm on my way,' Ness said.

Thank goodness for Ness. This took a heap of pressure off Matt and me, and it felt comforting to have such a close friend with us for the big event.

As Mike joined my parents at New Plymouth Airport to wait for the next flight to Auckland, Sophie, Matt, Ness and I converged on the labour ward at North Shore Hospital to prepare for our hurriedly organised caesarean. We must have looked a strange bunch all squeezed into the little birthing room, which had room for a bed, an armchair, a Swiss ball and not much else. We were full of nervous energy, giggling about how ridiculous we all looked in our surgical scrubs and making bad *Grey's Anatomy* jokes.

All I could think was: 'We're having a baby today!' I couldn't believe how fast everything was happening. A couple of hours ago we were getting ready to sip smoothies in a Ponsonby café. Sophie had arrived at hospital wearing heels, for goodness' sake!

It was time to head to theatre. Sophie was wheeled down the corridor while the three of us trailed nervously behind. I was anxious for Sophie and at the same time so excited.

I can see why they call it a theatre. The room where our baby boy was about to be born was huge, brightly lit and filled with a full cast of medical staff, all busily preparing for their roles. Sophie, the star of the show, was wheeled onto centre stage, her eyes shining with nerves, and the air was heavy with anticipation. There were a lot of people in the room, including Ammar, an anaesthetist, two midwives and several nurses and assistants.

I sat at Sophie's side, holding her hand, and Matt and Ness hovered in the background above her head. I couldn't help myself: I started to cry. The enormity of this was hitting me big-time. Sophie was so brave. She took slow, steadying breaths as the spinal block was administered. I could feel myself trembling, and Matt must have noticed because suddenly he was behind me, his steadying hands on my shoulders. All eyes were on our Soph.

It was a very odd feeling being in that theatre, knowing you're about to meet your son for the first time — a son you haven't carried in your tummy for nine months. I had delivered my two daughters in this same hospital after fifteen hours of labour, meeting them as a tired wreck of a human. This time I was neatly dressed, with my hair and makeup done: the scenarios could not have been more different.

A big white sheet blocked our view of what was happening, but Ammar gave a running commentary. 'I'm making the first incision now.' Things were moving at a calm pace and I think all of us were taking deep breaths as we waited for more information. Sophie and I kept our eyes on each other the whole time, both of us a little stunned.

At one point I noticed Soph had gone really pale and was wincing a bit from the tugging. I was worried she might pass out. I alerted the nurses and they swiftly upped the medication in her drip.

Then the adrenaline really kicked in when Ammar announced: 'You're going to meet this little boy very soon.'

At 1.42 p.m. on 9 August 2018, our son Lachlan Stephen France was born. He was held above the sheet in all his perfect, pink, miraculous, screaming glory. And at that moment I knew everything was going to be okay. The love I felt for that baby was instant and overwhelming. He looked and felt like mine.

'You did it,' I whispered to Sophie. 'You really did it, my girl.' I was in floods of tears by now, and overwhelmed with gratitude for my friend.

Ammar took Lachie around to Sophie so she could get a good look at him.

'Is he okay? He's okay, right?' Sophie was crying, too, and she urgently needed to know the baby she had carried was healthy and well.

'He's perfect, Soph, absolutely perfect,' I told her. 'You're amazing.'

'Go with him,' Sophie said through tears as the midwife took our baby to be checked on the other side of the room. I wanted to be with Lachie, desperate to take in every single part of him, but I couldn't leave Sophie's side.

'You go, Matt,' I said, not wanting to let go of Sophie's hand. In that moment, after all she had been through, she was my priority. I looked to where Matt was standing next to our little boy and saw he was beaming and full of emotion. Even Ammar had tears.

After he had been checked over, the midwife wheeled Lachie out of theatre, with Matt and I unable to take our eyes off him. I still hadn't held my boy and that ride up to the next floor felt like it took forever. I just wanted to wrap this bubba in my arms.

Leaving Sophie in theatre was extremely hard. I knew she had Ness to look after her, but it didn't feel right not being with her and to debrief what she'd been through. Soph must have sensed my hesitancy because she ordered me to follow my son. Ammar still needed to finish Soph's procedure, and she then needed to spend time in recovery.

Once we arrived in the ward it was finally my turn to get some much-needed skin-to-skin time with Lachie. I can say with certainty it was one of the most powerful moments of my life. I sat back in the La-Z-Boy chair, held him close and looked into the dark brown eyes of this tiny miracle. 'Hello, bubba. I'm your mama,' I whispered. I could have stayed that way for hours, just marvelling at this perfect little human.

I needn't have worried about our bond — I was instantly connected to this baby and everything felt just as it had with Juliette and Mackenzie. My feelings for him were so unequivocal that I couldn't believe I had been worried. His eyes were alert and he looked up at me as if to say 'I know you — what were you worrying about?'

And as I took in every part of him, I realised he was just as I had imagined him when I first started dreaming of my third child. He had a dark head of hair, dark eyes and gorgeous olive skin. He looked a lot like Stephen. He seriously looked heaps like my brother Stephen.

It was about an hour before Sophie was wheeled back into the ward, but it felt like an eternity. I badly needed to know that she was okay and I kept asking Matt to ring Ness to check on her.

She was pale and a little in shock when we finally saw her again. She had been very cold in recovery, so they had blown up a silver blanket with a hot pump to warm her up. Her low blood pressure also meant she had to stay in recovery longer. She was pumped full of drugs: a spinal block for the operation, morphine for the pain, and hormone medication to stop her milk from coming in. She was trying to be brave, but there was no escaping the fact she was sore and her emotions were all over the place.

'Meet Lachie,' I said, showing him to her again. It was an incredibly emotional moment. Sophie looked down at the little boy who only that morning had been kicking away inside her, and began to cry as she stroked his head. She wasn't ready to hold him.

'They're happy tears,' she insisted, but I knew they were more than that. I had known this incredible woman for over twenty years and I could tell she was hurting.

We spent the next couple of hours sitting quietly together in the recovery room, waiting for Mike and my parents to arrive.

There is no guidebook for surrogacy and none of us quite knew how we were supposed to act. Should I leave Sophie to sleep and take Lachie to another room, or would she rather have him here? Did she want time on her own with him? Was it good or bad for her to have this little baby near her? Was she sadder than we had expected?

I had no idea so I sat quietly, hoping the answers would become clearer.

I gave Lachie his first bottle, which he guzzled back, and Matt and I changed him into the little blue merino sleeping gown and matching hat and booties that we had picked out for him when all this was just a faraway dream.

Mike arrived, and so did Mum, Dad and Kirsty. Mum was crying before she even made it into the room. She headed straight for Sophie. My friend hadn't done this just for me, she'd done it for my entire family, and I'm sure seeing Mum's reaction would have made it clear how much this meant to all of us.

Our new baby was *fine* — swaddled tightly, a tummy full of milk and sound asleep in his little bassinet. It was Sophie we focused on now. She was at the centre of all our thoughts because it was she who had had the operation, and had carried a baby she had just given away.

The plan we had all agreed on was for Sophie to stay on at North Shore Hospital with Mike to recover while Matt and I took Lachie to Birthcare in Auckland City. But when that moment came, I was worried about leaving her. I could tell Soph was struggling. She didn't admit it at that point, but I found out later she felt worse than she had expected to, and was upset because it wasn't how she wanted to feel. Hormones aren't something you can plan for or control when it comes to having a baby, and hers were raging.

'We don't have to go tonight,' I told her. 'Please let us stay.'

If it would help her to have Lachie nearby that night, then that's what we would do. 'We can get another bed and I'll stay here with you.' I seriously didn't mind what we did — I just wanted what was best for her.

But Sophie was adamant — we were to go and bond with Lachie as planned. Mike was there and I got the impression he felt Soph could do with some space to rest and recover. So we packed up our stuff, kissed Sophie goodbye and took our little boy across to the other side of the city. Leaving Sophie behind in the hospital was one of the hardest, most confronting parts of the entire surrogacy journey. I cried and cried as Matt drove us away.

Our healthy little boy was strapped safely into his car seat and he was everything we had ever dreamed of, but my thoughts lingered with my best friend.

Matt reached over and squeezed my hand for reassurance.

The next four days were incredibly gritty for both Sophie and me. She was caught off-guard by her feelings of loss, and I was hit by another wave of anxiety and guilt. We'd had the perfect surrogacy scenario, but even so we were not protected from or prepared for the emotional fallout.

It was lovely being cocooned at Birthcare with our new baby and the support of the midwives, but I didn't sleep much that first night, and nor did Sophie back in the hospital. We kept our promise to communicate openly, so we texted each other constantly.

I told her how anxious I was not knowing how to make her feel better, and she told me she felt lonely now she was no longer pregnant. She hadn't expected to feel that way. She had thought that handing Lachie over would be the easy part, but the reality of giving birth to a baby who was not her own had knocked her around. It wasn't that she wanted to keep him — that had never crossed her mind, and she didn't regret what she had done. It didn't help that she was in a birthing ward, surrounded by joyous new mothers and crying babies. In hindsight, it would have been much better for her to be shifted to a general ward to recover.

North Shore Hospital is only a twenty-minute drive from Parnell, where Birthcare is housed in a grand old brick building at the foot of the Domain, but the distance between us felt like a gulf. It felt all wrong being apart; I just wanted to see her. I didn't have a bloody clue what was the best thing for her. Was Sophie insisting we stay at Birthcare because that's what she wanted — or was it for our sakes? Should I have ignored her and driven back with Lachie? I was so torn.

Things remained highly charged for the next few days. Lachie was oblivious, of course, and it seemed to us we had been sent an angel baby because he was so utterly content from the moment he arrived. This was incredibly reassuring, because if he had been unsettled I know I would have translated that as him being unhappy about being with us. Surrogacy, I was learning, is an emotional tightrope.

After two nights at Birthcare it was time to take Lachie home to start our new life as a family of five. The girls had visited him every day and were as besotted as we were — the fights had already begun over who got to hold him first and for the longest.

But before heading home we had an important detour to make. Sophie and Mike had also left the hospital that day and were staying in an Airbnb we had booked them in Takapuna. Sophie needed somewhere to recover for the next few days so they decided to make it a family holiday, with her parents bringing Bella and Theo up to join them.

I practically sprinted to the front door when we pulled up at the house.

It was an unseasonably beautiful day: the sun was shining, with a bright blue sky. Mike opened the door and I made a beeline for Soph, who was inside on the couch, sandwiched between her children, who had arrived earlier that morning. I gave her the longest hug we've ever had, and man it was so good to see her. She was still a little sore but looked so much better in herself, and assured me she was doing great and feeling happier now she had Bella and Theo with her. The colour was back in her cheeks and she was smiling, and in that moment we both knew that everything was going to work out. It was such a relief. I had worked myself into a state about her, but there she was, back with her kids and feeling content.

My parents arrived at the Airbnb with Juju and Mickey, and everyone was so happy and excited to be in the presence of this new baby. He was passed around like a parcel, absolutely smothered in love. I felt, and still feel, so happy to share him, because he is a special gift for both of our families.

Bubbles were poured, and everywhere I looked I saw love.

Sophie and I sat together on the sofa watching our families celebrate the new life that lay in front of us.

'Can you believe this has happened?' she whispered. 'We actually did it.'

Life is
for living

Lachie was our son. There was never any doubt.
Biologically, emotionally, the way he looked, the way
he acted — in every possible way he slotted into our
world as if he was always meant to be. Except he wasn't our
son. Until the adoption was finalised, just before Christmas

2018 and four months after his birth, Lachlan Stephen France was the legal child of Sophie and Michael Braggins.

It made sense with Sophie — she carried him, after all — but Mike? It made no sense. I had spent enough time getting worked up early on in the process over the ridiculously outdated laws that govern the surrogacy process, so I tried not to let Lachie's legal status worry me too much now that he was here. But it was a niggling frustration. What if we wanted to take him overseas? We would have had to get a special dispensation. What if he had needed urgent medical treatment? Sophie and Mike would have had to give permission. Technically, if Sophie and Mike suddenly changed their minds and decided they wanted to keep him, in the eyes of the law they would have had every right.

It was unsettling for Sophie, too. She deserved to be set free from the legal responsibility for a child who wasn't hers. It made zero sense that we had to adopt a baby who was 100 per cent biologically our child!

It took a frustratingly long time to get through the form-filling legal requirements and Oranga Tamariki visits. When the date was set for our hearing at the Family Court to sign it off, Matt and I decided to make an occasion out of it. We dressed Lachie up in a little shirt and suspenders for his big moment in front of the judge. It was merely a formality, but it felt significant.

The adoption approval was granted in less than a couple

of minutes, and finally Lachie was ours in every sense, and it signified the end of this extraordinary journey. We had the birth certificate with our names on to prove it.

At home, on a shelf above the desk in our office, sits a wooden box. It's there for Lachie when he's older and contains a little treasure chest of mementos from our surrogacy journey. In the box is a hospital bracelet that reads BABY OF SOPHIE BRAGGINS, and his original birth certificate, on which Sophie and Mike are named as his parents. There are photos of Sophie when she was pregnant with him, and pictures of him freshly delivered in the operating theatre. There are photos of him, Sophie and me together.

There are also folders heaving with documents from the surrogacy process, but who knows if he'll ever bother reading those! If he does, he'll see just what went into his creation, and I hope he'll always feel special knowing how badly we wanted him and what his 'Aunty Willow' did to make it happen.

Lachie is our child, but his relationship with Sophie is hugely important to Matt and me, and we take the responsibility of nurturing that relationship seriously. We live in different cities, which makes it harder, but we make sure we see one another often. We have a WhatsApp group where we're in touch most days, sharing photos and chatting about the minutiae of our lives. We go on shared family holidays, and all of our children think of each other as special cousins. Lachie is only three but he understands that he grew in Aunty

Willow's tummy, and I hope that as he gets older he'll realise how special that is.

Watching Sophie and Lachie together is the most heart-warming thing. Maybe I'm imagining it, but I'm sure he gravitates towards her. He's completely at ease in her company and freely gives her cuddles as if he knows she's somehow special to him. He's been that way since he was tiny.

I still get teary sometimes when I think about the fact that I now have a third child and it's all down to having such a selfless, incredible friend. Sometimes, out of the blue, I'll send Soph a text along the lines of 'I can't believe you did this for us, I'm just looking at Lachie and it still blows my mind.'

At some point I simply had to accept there was nothing I could ever do to adequately thank Sophie for what she did for us. I have come to a place of acceptance that she did it because she loves us and wanted to help us. It was an extraordinary gift of love that cannot be repaid except in love.

We marked Lachie's birth and her role in it by having a beautiful ring made for her with a peridot, which is the stone of Lachie's birth month. She wears it every day and I hope that when she looks down at that ring she feels proud of what she has done. I hope she understands the joy and love and healing it has brought to my whole family. I know she does.

Mum always hoped grandchildren would be part of her life. My children and Kirsty's new baby, William, have brought her so much joy, and they have developed a special bond just as close as she has with her own children. Despite Mum's incredible ability to press on with life despite all her setbacks, she would often joke about her bad luck. 'I probably won't be around to meet my first grandchild,' I remember her saying when I was in my early twenties. But look at her now — she's the centre of the universe for those four grandchildren.

I never intended this book to be a woe-is-me tale, because I have an amazing life and I know I am incredibly lucky. But grief is a funny thing, because almost twenty years after Stephen's death I can still be hit with an overwhelming sadness when I least expect it. People say time is a healer, but I'm not sure. Time is a healer, but it doesn't mean those pangs of grief ever stop completely.

I was reading an article recently by a New Zealand psychologist, Dr Lucy Hone. She specialises in resilience and wellbeing, and she also suffered the agonising loss of her twelve-year-old daughter Abi, who was killed in a road accident. Lucy wrote so powerfully and beautifully about her experience, and it obviously triggered something in me because suddenly I was overcome with my own grief. It was as if Stephen's death had just happened all over again. I closed my eyes and could see him; I could feel him. We were kids again. Then my mind travelled to my own little family and the awful thought of what if it ever happened again?

'You reach a point where you actively decide to keep pushing forward,' Mum said when I asked her how she survived. 'You're sad, but you keep going, and slowly, slowly it gets easier. The grief is there, but it's woven in with everything else.'

There are still tears, but there's so much happiness and laughter in between.

Mum says one of the things about experiencing so much tragedy is that you feel the happy times more intensely. You take *nothing* for granted when you have experienced great loss. Her love for her family spills out of every pore and she makes sure we all know how much we are loved.

We have a very grounded understanding of life and what is important. We try not to stress about the small things. We know what is worth valuing and what not to bother with.

Resilience is everything. Mum had no idea she had so much strength inside her, and she has taught all of us to believe in ourselves. If you had told a 23-year-old Wendy Street what was to come for her, she would have run for the hills. But she came through it all. She's incredibly strong, my mum.

She refuses to be bitter, because, despite what she's been through, she knows there are others who have it worse. She has her family; sure, some members are missing, but those who are here make her so happy.

She never got the chance to take Stephen to Disneyland so that's her big dream now, to take her grandchildren to the Happiest Place on Earth. 'As soon as borders reopen, we're off!' she says, as the Covid-19 global pandemic grinds on. She moves with the urgency and intent of someone who knows life can change at any moment.

We always knew our baby Lachie would be special, but none of us could have imagined the impact of his arrival on our family. If Stephen's death is one defining moment in my life, Lachie's birth is another — it's the point at which our family felt complete. He looks like Stephen and he acts like him, and it feels like a comforting link to the little brother I lost.

It's Lachie's first birthday and we're at the local church in Devonport for his christening. A beautiful, dappled morning light is filtering in through the stained-glass windows and it reminds me of our wedding day.

Sophie and Mike are standing at the front of the church with Matt and me. I'm holding Lachie, who's looking around wondering what all the fuss is about. Sophie and Mike are his godparents of course, and it feels special to be honouring them in this way.

Everyone who played a part in bringing Lachie into the world is here, and it feels so wonderful to reflect with them all on everything that has happened in the past year.

I look out and see Mum in the front row. Dad is clasping her hand and she's weeping. She feels close to God in here, which means she feels close to Lance, Tracy and Stephen.

The christening is over and we're walking out of the church. 'Are you okay?' I ask.

'I am so happy because Lachie is our special prize,' she says. 'He wasn't meant to be here but he is, and he was always waiting for you, Toni. He'll be your special boy forever; God will make sure of it.'

She says God, but she means Stephen. In Mum's eyes, Lachie is a gift from Stephen, and a sign that he's there and he's waiting for her. She doesn't fear death, and nor does my dad.

On Good Friday, five years after he died, Stephen appeared in front of Dad in the milking shed. He was surrounded by a golden light and he smiled and walked towards him. Dad was euphoric. He's back — my boy is back! Dad stood there, tears pouring down his cheeks, desperate to hug his son but unable to move, knowing the boy in front of him wasn't touchable.

Stephen was happy, smiling and emanating love as he told Dad: 'I'm okay, and it's not your fault.'

Epilogue

People ask me all the time about surrogacy, which shows there's a lot of interest out there, but very little helpful information available. I am always at pains to make it clear that the journey is far riskier and more complicated than my own experience suggests.

My surrogacy story sounds a bit like a fairytale. We were two families who loved and trusted each other, it all went smoothly, we got our beautiful little boy, and everyone went on with their lives.

But for many people the journey is nowhere near as smooth.

The unfortunate reality is that the current law governing surrogacy in New Zealand fails to give either party (the surrogate or the intending parents) adequate legal protection. Each party is entirely at the mercy of the other, and if things go wrong someone is likely to end up devastated.

In the first five months of 2021 there have been two news stories about surrogacy arrangements in New Zealand that ended badly. The first involved a couple whose surrogate changed her mind during the pregnancy. After a lengthy court battle the two parties are now in the unimaginable position of sharing custody of the baby.

The second story is equally heartbreaking and involves a surrogate mother terminating a pregnancy without the intending parents' knowledge. There were reported mental health issues for the surrogate, and I feel for her, but this arrangement should never have been signed off in the first place. The fact that the intending parents had no legal rights over this unborn baby is another indication of serious flaws in our current system.

When it became clear to me that New Zealand's surrogacy

laws need urgent reform, I joined the call for change. I didn't set out to shake things up, but I was encouraged when Prime Minister Jacinda Ardern responded to a post I made on Instagram after Lachie's adoption. She agreed that reform was needed, and, not long afterwards, the Law Commission announced a review of surrogacy law.

I was contacted in early 2021 and asked to make a submission based on my own experience, which of course I'm happy to do. I'm relieved and delighted the lawmakers have finally acknowledged that change is needed.

In my submission I plan to argue for greater protection for intending parents. Currently there is nothing preventing the surrogate from changing her mind and deciding to keep a child that is biologically not hers. Greater protection is also needed for the surrogate, so she cannot be saddled with the baby she has carried if the intending parents change *their* minds for whatever reason.

But it's the adoption side of surrogacy that most urgently needs change. The fact that Sophie and Mike had full legal rights over Lachie until he was four months old, while we had none, was very upsetting and felt completely wrong. It astounds me that the biological parents are placed in this position, with no way of legally progressing the agreed adoption if the surrogate decides she wants to keep the child herself.

It's a messy, risky business, and my advice to people

considering surrogacy is to be very wary until there are law changes. Go into it with your eyes wide open. Follow the official channels, get good legal advice, take the counselling sessions seriously and, most of all, if you have doubts at any stage before there is a pregnancy, consider putting the plan on hold.

L achie is now three years old and life is great. It's crazy busy, but I am determined to take in every moment with my last baby. We're here, we're happy and we're healthy — what more could we ask?

I've been in remission from Churg-Strauss for four years. I've been warned that it will probably return one day but I try not to live in fear of it. I've deliberately taken the approach that I'm going to enjoy being well, because what's the point of ruining the joy of what we have now by stressing about what may arise in the future?

If the Churg-Strauss does come back, at least I will know this time what I'm dealing with, and what to do. I hope I never have to have those steroid infusions again, but if I do, it will be in the knowledge that they will make me better.

I still take a small amount of steroid medication every day. I would love to one day be drug-free but my specialist says it's unlikely, and I'm okay with that if it keeps me alive. I know when I'm overdoing things because my body sends me signals, I have to be on the lookout for signs of flare-ups such as eczema or asthma, which mean something is out of whack and I need to slow down.

As a naturally on-the-go type of person I have had to really work at learning to live at a slower pace. I used to think that sitting down and doing nothing was a bad thing. I had to be constantly busy — doing something, going somewhere, on the move all the time. It has taken me a long time to realise it's okay to chill out. I have learnt — the hard way — the importance of rest.

This stuff doesn't come easily for me. Friends and family are always telling me I need to get better at saying no, and I know they're right. But really, I don't think I'm different to any other working mum. It's normal to always be on the go at this stage of life, right? The work–life juggle is just that: a constant juggle. Some days or weeks go well; at other times it seems to be a case of running from one drama to another.

My main objective is to be there for my kids when they need me. Even though life gets insanely busy at times, I am determined to be as much of a hands-on mother as I can. I'm writing this at the start of winter, which means netball season is upon us. I am coaching both the girls' teams, which involves wrangling twenty girls aged six to nine, with weekly training sessions and running the show on game days.

You'll find me there at the courts, sneakers on, whistle around my neck, and I absolutely love it. It's possible I'm a little too much like my dad, though, because I take it super-seriously. As soon as a game ends, I'm already thinking ahead to next week's match, contemplating the competition, planning which positions the kids will play and making sure everyone is happy.

After four years in commercial radio (first at The Hits and now Coast) I feel I've really got the hang of it, and I love the warmth, informality and humour of the breakfast slot. I'll always be ambitious, but I am certainly not out looking for the next role or the next step up the career ladder. Right now, there's nowhere else I'd rather be. Yes, it's brutal getting up at 4 a.m., but the hours work well for family life and I'm happy that I see the kids as much as I do.

I am also incredibly grateful for the television opportunities that have continued to come my way since leaving my permanent *Seven Sharp* role. Hosting the 2021 America's Cup for TVNZ was a career highlight, and, even though it was full-on, being part of Team New Zealand's victory is something I'll never forget. There were tough parts — like ad-libbing for three hours when sailing was postponed! — but the thrill of being part of the action never gets old.

At the time of writing, we're in the final stages of planning coverage of the Tokyo Olympics. For someone who started life as a sports reporter, it doesn't get any better than fronting international events like these, and the fact that it's all happening during a global pandemic just adds to the significance.

My family has been dealt some huge challenges, for sure, but I feel so lucky to be where I am today. I am filled with love and gratitude for everyone around me who has helped make that possible.

Acknowledgements

There are lots of people I would like to thank who have helped contribute to this book.

First of all, to Mum and Dad, who encouraged me to write it in the first place. You were right, the process was cathartic, and although it was tough at times rehashing painful memories, I'm glad I did it. Thank you for your openness and willingness to talk about such deeply personal and painful aspects of your life, I have no doubt it will help other parents who have also lived with the horror of losing a child.

In typical Sophie style, my bestie was all for me writing this book. To Soph, Mike and the entire Braggins family, thank you for allowing me to detail our surrogacy journey. I hope this will serve as a keepsake to remind you of the incredible thing you have done for me and our family. I will make sure Lachie gets to read all about it when he's old enough.

For the last eighteen months, I have worked closely with Sophie Neville, who helped me write *Lost and Found*. She has done most of the heavy lifting. Thank you for your patience and perseverance especially during lockdown. It's no easy task trying to write a book with three kids and while home schooling! Your empathy and tone in dealing with the tough topics is so appreciated.

To my husband Matt, thank you for being a constant sounding board, and chief kid wrangler when I was 'on a roll'.

To Dean Buchanan, thank you for taking care of all the logistics for me (especially during those crazy months when the America's Cup was on!), and for easing my concerns about writing a book initially. Your feedback and encouragement were invaluable.

And lastly, I would like to acknowledge publisher Michelle Hurley, Leonie Freeman, and the entire Allen & Unwin team. Thank you for the opportunity to tell my story. Thank you for being interested, for being so easy to deal with, and for making this process enjoyable.